D0300831

In Memory of my late husband Owen who taught me wisdom and how to see the beauty of each new day and to never take any blessings no matter how small for granted – thankyou.

Also to my two children Sophia and Hugh who gave me a reason to get up each morning during those dark days of depression and despair. You both continue to inspire others with your strength.

ACKNOWLEDGMENTS

I would like to thank and appreciate all the following people who have inspired me with their personal stories of the paranormal. They are as follows:

To my wonderful mother Philomena thank you for a lifetime of love, nurturing and a profound belief in me.

To my mother-in-law Kitty Walsh who has been a source of strength and love to myself and two children throughout those early bleak days to the present. Thank you.

To my two children Sophia and Hugh for their endurance and courage.

To Patrick Treacy for you wisdom, compassion and encouragement along my journey towards recovery. Thank you.

For my family especially my sister Gabrielle and brother-in-law Bill for your kindness, support and loving understanding.

And my brother Desmond for your consistent presence and concern throughout my loss.

To Patricia Nolan counsellor and friend thank you for your loving assistance and inspirational guidance during those early days of darkness and despair.

To James Van Praagh for being a resounding Spiritual Beacon for my personal growth and a compassionate human being to so many people around the globe – Thank you.

To Geri O'Connor a wonderful friend and such a wise companion. Thank you also.

To Victor and Wendy Zammit for your tireless and wonderful work compiling evidence of the afterlife in abundance in your weekly reports to the world.

And finally to my husband Owen and father Joseph Desmond in the Spirit world who came to me through my dreams with their powerful messages of loving guidance and enlightenment which brought about this book. Without your help it would never have been written. I hope to be continuously enlightened and inspired by more messages to come.

"The Illusion of Mortality" is much, much more than a book about a woman's devastating journey through grief, it is a pure food for the soul. We often question why bad things happen to us and after reading this treat, it puts everything into perfect perspective. From Intuition and dreams, to the depth and scope of a father's love, this book is a manual to live by. Phyllis Walsh is not only a gifted teacher, author and counsellor, but takes what at times can be a heady and unrelatable subject and brings it right down to earth for us to ponder the innate truths of our being. Thank you Ms. Walsh for sharing your story with us and being daring enough to perhaps heal the world."

James Van Praagh.
NY Times Best-selling author,
International Spiritual Medium.

CONTENTS

SAYING GOODBYE

I was a wife and mother of two living a normal everyday life when back in February 2006 the life I knew and was very comfortable with was changed forever. At that time I thought life for me had indeed finished. Here I will try to tell my story as it unfolded as best as I can. This is only my story but I hope you will find it as intriguing and as interesting as I found the events which followed to be. Sadness and adversity unfortunately effect us all at some stage or other in our lives. It is just part of the human condition that we will all experience good times, amazing times, hard times, and devastating times. It is the latter time which brought about this book and how I found the tools and resources to come through the most ravaging turmoil which is the heart wrenching trauma of loosing someone you love dearly and completely. The morning of February the 12th, 2006 dawned like any other. There was nothing unusual or different in any aspect about that day. However, the events which occurred later in the early evening have changed my life and that of my family forever. My young vibrant husband of just 43 died suddenly. There was no warning, no chance to say Goodbye, no anticipation or expectedness of this sudden outcome. He just died as quietly and peacefully as he had lived his life. My two children at the time were three and nine and I thought my own life was over as well. How did this happen to us?

These things only happen to 'other people.' But I had now become one of those 'Other People.' Now it was at my doorstep and my path to recovery was not to begin for some years later. However, I soon came to realise that although my husband had gone physically, he was still with me and my children. This realisation did not happen for some time later. I had the immediate aftermath of trying to tell my little three year old boy that his daddy was with Holy God. A concept that no three year old can either understand or relate to. And should not have to. He just wanted his daddy back and was oblivious to the concept of finality. The finality of loosing someone you love physically. His age was in itself a blessing, but my daughter took it much worse. We were all present when he died that night two days before Valentines's Day. The events which later followed have given me a new resolve and a knowledge that we are never abandoned by our loved ones when they physically leave. I hope by my sharing the following fascinating experiences it will give a glimmer of hope to anyone bereaved. To know that there is life beyond this life and that we will all be reunited one day again.

Last family holiday taken with Owen and the children just seven months before his death in February 2006.

Part 1

When Life Changes Us We Can Choose To Change Our Life

Chapter 1
WHEN SOMEONE WE LOVE DIES

Life is eternal, and love is immortal, and death is only a horizon, and a horizon is nothing save the limit of our sight – Rossiter Worthington Raymond.

This book is for anyone who has lost a loved one and is curious about what happens after our physical bodies die. Unfortunately death is part of life and is a natural conclusion to the physical state. It is something that we do not like to talk about. It is the finality of death which we find disturbing and difficult to deal with so we rather not until it touches our own lives. We will each of us at some time loose a loved one. Depending on the relationship to that person impacts directly on the strength of grief we suffer as a result of that loss. Be it a spouse, a relative, a sibling, a child, your neighbour, each has its own type of hit. But some losses are relatively speaking deeper and harder than others. For me, loosing my young husband suddenly was like being hit by a freight train at huge speed. This traumatic life event had ambushed me with a might I was left reeling from for years. Death no matter which way we try to dress it up or use euphonisms, is by far the hardest of human experience to deal with. We all go about our daily routine trying to do the best we can with what we have. Quite a lot of the time taking what and who we have around us for granted. However, like a lot of things in life it is only when we loose something or someone do we start to realise what and who we had so blessed in our lives. Simple things we all take for granted like our hearing, our eyesight, the ability to get up and walk those of us who are lucky enough to do so. Not to have any pain. Who can do what they want, when they want without thinking. But all these abilities which we never pay a moments notice to are all in of themselves blessings in abundance.

DISTRAUGHT: Loving husband and father of two had entered Gerry Ryan competition

Agony at death of dream holiday dad

BY MARK HILLIARD

THE heartbroken wife of a romantic would-be radio competition winner, has told how her husband died just hours before trying to secure a dream holiday on the Gerry Ryan Show.

Loving Eoin Walsh (42) passed away on Sunday night leaving behind him a distraught wife and a young family.

He had entered a competition to win a holiday in one of the world's most romantic get-aways but instead hopes of paradise turned to tragedy.

COMPETITION

"He was only 42 and he was dead in three minutes," his grief-stricken wife Phyllis said of his sudden death.

"I still can't believe it. I still feel like he's going to walk through the door any minute now. Everybody loved Eoin, he was such a wonderful person."

He had been one of thousands of people who entered last week's competition on the Gerry Ryan show.

Contestants had to repeat lines from some of their favourite romantic films in a bid to secure the Valentine's Day trip to Paris, Casa Blanca, New York or Rio de Janeiro.

For his part, dad of two Eoin had found his way to the final with his version of the film Sweet Charity.

But his fun-loving world was brought crashing to its knees on Sunday when the young father died of a suspected heart attack.

Now his wife Phyllis must console their two children Sophia (9) and Hugh (3).

"We were having an Indian takeaway and he had a curry and a glass of wine," she recalled.

"He brought his food into the living room and he was just sitting down when he said, 'This is lovely, sitting here relaxing, talking to you'.

"Then all of a sudden he slid down the settee and his breathing got very laboured."

Phyllis then ran for help, phoning an ambulance and staying on the line in a desperate attempt to give them vital information on his condition.

Sophia remained by her father's side trying to take his pulse and screaming that she loved him.

STRONGER

"I don't think that is something that a nine-year-old should ever have to go through but she's great," her mother said.

"She's way ahead of her years and she was stronger than I was. She's constantly asking if I'm OK. By the time I got downstairs he was gone."

Instead of celebrating a potential Valentine's holiday, Phyllis and her family are now struggling to come to terms with Eoin's death.

The music teacher who taught children the piano in Kilmacud, south Dublin, has left a tormented family behind and Phyllis must now attempt to explain to his young son why he would not be coming home again.

"He was 6ft 6in and when he walked into a room it lit up," she remembered.

LOVING COUPLE: But Phyllis Walsh is now mourning the death of her husband Eoin

Owen had been a finalist in a competition on one of Ireland's most popular morning radio program. As a result his sudden death brought with it alot of publicity.
Picture courtesy of the Herald Newspaper.

TRAGEDY OF RADIO SHOW HUBBY

A POPULAR young music teacher who was supposed to take part in a Valentine's Day competition on Gerry Ryan's radio show has died suddenly.

Eoin Walsh (42) was planning to win the holiday of a lifetime for his wife and two young children — but he died of a suspected heart attack on Sunday night.

"He was dead within three minutes," said his heartbroken widow Phyllis.

■ SEE PAGE 9

SUDDEN DEATH: Eoin and Phyllis Walsh

Valentine's finalist (42) dies in front of wife and two children

Talk to anyone who is blind, or deaf or has lost the ability to use a body part. They will soon put all of these into a profound perspective. On the other hand to loose a Soulmate, a child, or a very close friend is quite plainly – horrific. There is no other word. Not alone have you lost that special person but you now have to deal with the aftermath of no longer having that loved one in your life. I liken it to switching on a television and the picture is only in black and white. No matter how much you fiddle around with the switches, you can only see the images without colour. I use this analogy because that was how I saw life around me following the death of my husband. Life had lost its glow, its substance. The colour was turned off in and around my existence. I was in robotic mode. Doing perfunctory things. Daily jobs which had to be done. Dragging my feet as I tried to do them and make sense of my situation. I found myself in that pit of despair a lot of people find themselves when in the midst of a bereavement. People rallied around for awhile, but then they started to dissipate and go back into their own lives. And rightly so. But my life had finished. Certainly the life which I knew to be had indeed finished. I never would have thought back then that any semblance of a new life would ever emerge. But this is exactly why I needed to write this book. For those of you who are entering into the journey of grief or know somebody close who is, I want to say to you that life will go on and that you will emerge into a new life with new possibilities. I did it and I am just beginning. So can you. I want to give hope and encouragement to others who were like me. Do not give up. The analogy of the caterpillar turning into the wonderful butterfly. Yes, in a sense the caterpillar 'dies' but a new life emerges. I have found from my own experience and from other people that situations happen in our life for a reason – a specific purpose. We may not see it like that at the time, but eventually the reason will unfold. 'What does not break us down, builds us up.' We may be like the walking wounded in the begining, and our emotional scars may not be obvious to all, but we *will* be stronger in time.

AWAKENINGS

The first year following my husband's passing was one which was clouded in a dense fog. This was the fog of adjustment, disbelief, denial and finally trying to find my footing again in my new life. I was still a mother, and still *felt* like a wife. But reality told me I no longer was. We define ourselves by who and what we are. The jobs we have, the things we do in life. However, half of my identity as I knew it to be was no more. You see I was no longer a wife – but a *widow*. I always disliked that word *Widow*. It has a negative connotation of a kind. It conjures up a depressing picture of a sad lonely woman whose life has somehow ended. And in a sense it has. For me being a young widow, I was beginning to identify with this image. Due to my extreme grief and emotional pain there were times when I wished my life had ended. But I had two young children to raise, a three year old little boy and a nine year old girl. Added to this my little boy has special needs and that fact took on an even different and deeper agenda. Today with the passage of time, he has become one of my best helpers and teachers in who I am. It seemed back then like too much to carry. But then God gives us the burdens he knows we are able to deal with. Sometimes I do question this. Because when you hear of people who for example have lost children though either murder, war and or other dreadful scenarios, it is difficult to apply this notion. Some people may be better than others to shoulder some of life's unfortunate handouts. None of us ask for the negative situations which come into our lives. Most of the time we have no choice. However we must deal with disasters when and where they arise as best as we can. Each of us has our own coping skills and personal strategies to manage life's adversities. But I had no choice either at that time. I was a single parent whether I liked it or not. My husband had died, and yes I was a young widow.

My days back then a lot of the time were without much clarity but I managed to get through them. My husband used to say when he was alive, that if I was going through a bad time, not to take it one day at a time, but to take it one *hour* at a time. And I would say this to any of you who are going through any particular difficulty. Just take it an *hour* at a time. Bite size pieces. In the beginning of our marriage after our daughter Sophia was born, we suffered the trauma of loosing three babies through miscarriage. Each loss was as difficult and as hard to come to terms with. And one miscarriage does not in itself prepare you for the loss of the next. Each one is different and unique. It was a big lesson for us both in grief management. I used to say to people that I could give a master class on loss, and now I certainly could. But somehow we both made it through those dark lonely days of loss and adjustment. Unbeknown to me at that time, they were the lessons to pave the way for my biggest hurdle to come. But looking back on those bleak and lonely months, I noticed that some new and wonderful people were beginning to enter my life. People who I would never have met if my husband were still alive today. However, they were blessings in disguise. Some were people who had experienced the same or similar loss as myself. The only difference was that they were further up the road of recovery than I was. They were therefore able to impart glimmers of hope and inspiration to me when my spirit was broken and in pieces. I do believe that the human Spirit can be incredibly strong. We only have to hear stories of the concentration camps and the atrocities the survivors witnessed. Somehow they found the strength against all the odds to move forward and live their lives in society having lost everything. So within my own sadness, I tried to focus on others misfortune and felt that if they could cope and surmount their immense difficulties I certainly could do the same.

I began to focus on what good still remained within my immediate surroundings. I had my children, my mother, my family and good friends around me. Instead of seeing only what I had lost, I tried to shift my perception towards what and who I *still had* in my life. This I found to be an important lesson in moving on more effectively. I noticed very subtly that there were 'moments' in the days ahead that gave me strength and hope. I would describe them like ' small rays of sunshine' amist the darkness. I had a wonderful counsellor who came into my life, who is now a very good friend. She herself had also lost a young husband years before and had also been left with a three year old little boy to raise. She used to tell me to try and give myself little 'treats' or just something small to look forward to throughout the day. She had called them *night lights*. In time she assured me that these *night lights* would get brighter and illuminate the darkness. The pain will start to dissipate slowly at first, almost indiscernably. But it is a process. And like all processes, it takes time. It has to evolve. Whether we like it or not, despite whatever situation we find ourselves in life will take us forward. Like a fast flowing stream, it moves on over bumpy terrain sometimes smooth, and we are like the untethered boat that *goes with the flow*. We can decide to fight it or move along with it and start to navigate the waters of life the best we can. In the beginning, the analogy I would use is someone in a small boat with no oars to hand. Finding ones self being swung around whirlpools and knocked against banks, but then with the kindness of strangers and human *angels* I was given strong oars to steer the boat of life safely and with direction without the chaos of leaving everything to chance. We can all find ourselves in the river of life without an anchor or an oar to centre us at tragic times. But if we look carefully, and listen keenly, we are indeed sent help to stand along side us.

I will later talk of fascinating synchronities which I encountered. There is no such thing as coincidence. Everything that happens, happens exactly at the time it is meant to happen and that goes for circumstances and meeting the people we meet. Even chance meetings can change one's life. I have had many such encounters which have enriched and changed my general perspective. Some may only last moments others longer. But they can be quite powerful. There is a beautiful poem which illustrates such encounters and how meaningful they can impact on our lives. I will share it with you shortly but it gives me great consolation and acceptance when people have to say goodbye. I hope you too will take away the wisdom and the depth of the words. It may also particularly help when certain individuals leave our lives without giving us notice. Some stay with us for a fixed period of time, others only for a fleeting moment. But everyone has something to say and add to our existence. Everyone is precious, unique, and has a gift to offer the world. All we need to do is to listen. I came across the following beautiful poem depicting why people come and go from our lives at different stages. The author is unknown but the words are a stunning testimony to the various stages we can be touched by one another, and how compassionate human beings can truly be. The following words really helped me along my journey through bereavement. Enjoy the message which this conveys and hopefully you will find solace and peace in their meaning as well. Absorb the essence of each phrase.

People come into your life for a reason, a season or a lifetime. When you know which one it is you will know what to do for that person.
When someone is in your life for a REASON it is usually to meet a need you have expressed.
They have come to assist you through a difficulty to provide you with guidance and support.
To aid you physically emotionally or spiritually.
They may seem like a godsend and they are.
They are there for the reason you need them to be.
Then without any wrong doing on your part or at an inconvenient time
This person will bring the relationship to an end.
Sometimes they die. Sometimes they walk away.
Sometimes they are up and force you to take a stand.
What we must realize is that our need has been met our desire fulfilled their work is done.
The prayer you sent up has been answered and now it is time to move on.

Some people come into your life for a SEASON
because your turn has come to share grow or learn.
They bring you an experience of peace or make you laugh
They may teach you something you have never done
They usually give you an unbelievable amount of joy
Believe it, it is real. But only for a season
LIFETIME relationships teach you lifetime lessons
Things you must build upon in order to have a solid
emotional foundation.
Your job is to accept the lesson love the person and put
what you have learned to use in all other relationships
and areas of your life
It is said that love is blind but friendship is clairvoyant
Thankyou for being a part of my life
Whether you were a reason, a season or a lifetime.

Unknown Author.

I have also found wonderful wisdom in sayings, and lines from songs. Also Children can have such pure clarity and vision in their thinking. Wherever we can, accept and acknowledge that there are signs all around us trying to put us on the right path in life. We are all guided by unseen hands and in time they will be the sign posts to where we need to go to next in our lives.

I would like to say to family members and friends who are around the bereaved person is to guage if they wish to talk about their loved one who has passed. To acknowledge the person who has died. People feel bad enough trying to cope with the harrowing aftermath of bereavement. There really is nothing worse or upsetting for the person grieving then for family or friends to pretend that all is normal. By not saying anything about the deceased can to some seem a little dismissive and unfeeling. This certainly would not be intentional but when we are wounded emotionally, our perception can become warpted and clouded towards others around us. I know alot of the time people genuinely do not know what to say. So instead they say nothing. The bereaved want their loved one to be acknowledged even though they are out of sight. After all they existed, lived, loved, contributed, touched lives, helped and encouraged people when they were alive. They sustained people, so pay homage to their memory with your family and friends when you feel ready and strong enough to do so. It is all different and relative for each one of us. Celebrate their lives, talk about them. Remember the happy times, the funny times, the amazing times. But *talk* about them when you wish to express your loss, sadness etc. Everyone is different. Everything is relative. How long is a piece of string? Each one of us has our own mechanism of coping with grief. Some prefer to keep silent and remain in their own space for awhile. While others will want to talk adnauseam about their loss. People are as different emotionally as they are physically. Also the way we all internalize feelings vary immensely. I never knew how devastating grief could affect one's whole countenance and being. It impacts physically, emotionally, and psychologically. The metaphor of how long is a piece of string? You cannot give a definitive answer. It is as different and unique to all human beings. Just getting through a day can be a monumental task in of itself. Let your family and those close to you know if you want or do not want to talk about the person who has passed. Some people feel by not mentioning the person in your presence that it will not be an upset to you. For some the very opposite can be the case. Fine if that is the way you want it to be, but painfully frustrating if you feel their memory is being mildly erased to eleviate any uncomfortable atmosphere. It is the 'elephant in the room.' It is there. Huge. Everyone sees and feels it, but no one is making any reference to it. Lead the way, and others will take your lead and guidance from you.

People will sympatise with you but unless death has touched their lives it is hard for them to have a full empathetic connection with you. They may see but cannot *feel* or realise the emotional torture which deep grief brings. The 'elephant' will always be there, but hopefully with the passage of time, it will get smaller and less powerful. You will be able to find different ways to navigate around it when out with people. And one day you will look around and it will be but a distant memory. And here again I am referring to the awkward topic for some people with the issue of not being able to deal with a grieving individual and the enormity of their grief in company. In the chapters to follow, I will reveal several fascinating encounters which have helped me in my personal healing and recovery through grief. My story is a combination of bereavement and spirituality. How I came to find out how strongly connected and interlinked together these two elements are. These experiences came to me very early on after loosing my husband. From there on in a string of intriguing events made me witness that something extroadinary was starting to happen in my life. I hope you will gleen some consolation and enduring hope in what began to touch my own life. Experiences so amazing and wonderful that I felt stongly compelled to write this book. Because of them, and not despite them, I have been made stronger, more spiritual, more compassionate and extremely hopeful that 'we are only passing through here *this life,* that the BEST is yet to come ....

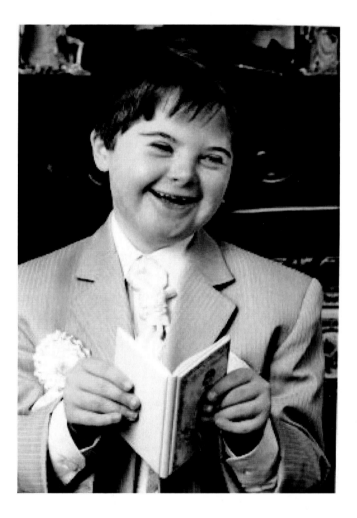

Hugh on his 'First Holy Communion' making the best of his special day and knowing his father was parenting very close by - but just in a different way.

Chapter 2

TOUCHED BY THE LIGHT

In Life's Sad moments, when things "fall Apart" it is to make room for Bigger and Better Things "To Come Together".

In this picture taken with my son you will see a pale misty hue beside me and across my face. This occured in a few pictures shortly after my husband passed

I was raised a Catholic and abided by the Catholic rules by going to Mass, saying my prayers and learning religion at school. I could never say that I had a *deep* faith, but I always felt that there was something greater and bigger than myself. A higher force, a Supreme Being, some figure of light beyond our human understanding. I never gave it much thought I must say. However, I accepted and took up the religious doctrine which was handed down to me by my parents, teachers and the religious people in the catholic church. However, I never grasped the concept of spirituality and anything spiritual until I was married and began having *unusual* and *interesting* events occur in my life. These events were very subtle at first. I must say in the beginning I thought perhaps it was only in my imagination. But I began to pay closer attention to what I was witnessing.

To begin with, two years into my marriage I had my daughter Sophia. Six weeks into the pregnancy I began bleeding very heavily and went for a scan. I was told that I would probably go on to loose the baby. But when the doctor left the room I stared at the screen seeing the tiny embryonic sack and thought I saw a little heartbeat. I will always remember there was a lovely little nurse with me in the room and I pointed this out to her. She said that it looked good but did not want to give me too much hope after what the doctor had just said to me. Well, the pregnancy did progress with extreme *morning* sickness which I had morning, noon, and night. Night time was the worst. I could keep nothing down as far as food was concerned. I just felt lousy for those months until finally the nausea dissipated and I began to feel normal again. Because the bleeding was quite severe at the beginning I was told that my daughter could have been a twin. And twins do run on my mothers side of the family. However, I was very grateful and relieved when on May the 2nd 1996, I gave birth to a beautiful little girl who was a determined fighter to get to this life to begin with. With a new baby and being a first time mum, I was trying to adjust to sleep deprevation and the business of looking after such a little being. She did not have any particular sleeping pattern for the first six months. Both my husband and I would barely get two to fours hours sleep at times. However, as time went on, the baby settled into a better sleeping routine and life continued along with a more peaceful degree of normality.

The first encounter I had with spirituality was to occur twelve months later when I found out we were expecting a second baby. There was great excitement and anticipation at the news. We were already thinking of names if it was a boy or a girl. We just continued on with our life and paving the way for our new addition. But that was all to change when one morning I began to bleed, just a little. I tried to tell myself that I had already experienced this with my first baby and she was strong and healthy. This was nothing like the episode I had then. Just a little spotting. Nothing to worry about. I remember thinking that perhaps I will not say anything to my husband. Don't worry him. He was busy getting ready for the day ahead. But something made me mention what had happened and I tried to be as casual and nonchalant as possible not to upset him. He thought differently and made me go immediately to the hospital to see that everything was fine with the baby. I was three months along. I must say at the time, I really was not very worried. I did not want to make a fuss. The medical team were so busy and I did not want to add to their work load. However, we were ushered into a small dark room where the equipment was ready to scan my tummy. There was not much talk. Just an awkward silence. And then the hollow bleep of the ultrasound machine began moving and searching. I never took my face off the nurse. She never said anything. Just kept keenly looking at the screen and then she asked me how far along I was. She looked back at the screen and I knew by her face that all was not good. It was my husband Owen who asked if the baby was alright. And she began to tell us that she was not able to find a heart beat. I remember hearing those words, but not taking in the enormity of them. My baby was fine she just needed to keep looking for the signs. But I could see the head, the tiny arms and legs and desperate for some positive movement from within, but nothing. My baby had died. I felt desolate. Miscarriage happens to *other* people. Not to us. But then why not us? But now I felt the carnage, the terrible sadness of loosing this little person who we had hoped would enter our lives. Shell shocked and numb we both made our way home.

I began trying to accept what had just happened. Our daughter was only fifteen months old when we lost our baby. The days went by with a heavy heart. I had recently entered a competition for 'Homemaker of the Year' and to my surprise became one of the finalists. There were ten of us left from a few thousand entrants. I should have felt good, but all I felt was a bleakness inside me. So I was to appear with one of our best broadcasters in one of dublin's famous theatres 'The Gaeity Theatre' and it was going to be televised! How was I going to do this with what had just happened. I was physically exhaused and emotionally shattered. I still had to go into hospital in a few days time. But a deep strength within pushed me to continue with the competition. It was just three days before I was due to go on stage that I was lying awake in my room one night. I will always remember it. Our room was in near darkness with the bedroom door opened just a little. The light from the landing was shining into our room so you could make out everything in the room. Sophia our fifteen month old at the time was sleeping between us, and my husband was sound asleep. I however, was anxious about appearing on television and wondering if I would have to pull out of the competition. What happened next amazed me. But it did happen. My fifteen month old baby woke up beside me and began staring intently at one side of our bedroom up at the ceiling. Very keenly and with a definite stare. Then she lifted her head and her eyes began to widen. She appeared to be following something. I continued to watch her look at and follow some unseen image above her. She began to wave and started to smile brightly. With this I tried to wake up my husband. He just saw the tale end of what I was witnessing. "Who are you waving at?" I asked her. She said " a baby". And I saw her wave and with her eyes tracking something unseen to me from one side of my bedroom to another. At this stage, she just lay back on the pillow and did not seem to be frightened or disturbed in any way. I knew however that a fifteen month old baby is incapable of deception. She *did* see something.

To her it appeared to be a normal and natural event. I kept on seeing her eyes widen with a delight as she raised her arms and began to wave with an eagerness one could just not ignore. Her whole countenance was animated. We were not privy to what she was seeing. But then we were not meant to be. This was only for her to see. I was wondering after just having lost my baby, if this was the baby she saw. Was she saying goodbye as her sibling was leaving this dimension? Who knows. But I will never ever forget that night. It is as clear to me now as it was when it happened nearly fourteen years ago. I felt that I was priviledged to have witnessed something so precious, so real, such a wonder to behold. But it was not for my eyes. I saw nothing at all. They say very young children can see things and events which we as adults are unable to see. Because they have recently left the spirit world they are still untouced by this life. So many parents have heard their children play with their 'imaginary friends'. To them they are real. To us it appears that they are acting out some great imagination. An imaginary friend who seems to interact with the child. But it is said that there is more to these imaginery friends. They are never frightened. They are always happy, content, never perturbed. It is a fascinating concept and it is a world wide occurence. Anyway, unbeknowns to me that was just the start of a string of intriguing events which was to continue in my life and up into the present time.

We all have a mindset, an in built mechanism of how we perceive things to be. This can be both a combinaton of environmental and our genetic predisposition. But this mindset can change. It is up to us which way it goes. I was a prisoner from the constraints which kept me from realizing my full potential after my husband died. My main constraint at that time was one of deep depression and desolation. It lasted for several years, but I was able to mask it from most people. Only those close to me truly knew the extent of my despair and they stood with me through thick and thin. I owe them so much. I so wanted to be released into the freedom of my full potential but was unable to find the tools or the energy for that matter to do so. We cannot be free until we know what shapes, governs, and directs our behaviour. And eventually our outcomes in life. Out thinking, our conditioning can be controlled by our paradigms. Our thoughts are fundamentally crucial to the quality of our life. We create our life. Paradigms are our mindset. They are themselves neutral. If they are positive, you will be a happier person. Your self-image and esteem will begin to improve. You will be able to deal with adversities in a more constructive and planned way. Conversely, negative paradigms will keep you stuck in your old ways of thinking. And because of this can be very limiting.

Reprogramming your mind will take you back on a journey into your past. Why do we think the way we do. Ask yourself that question. How do you react to change in your life? Do you panic? Do you question? Do you accept? Do you get angry? Or do you see some hidden opportunity perhaps lurking in the wings of your life beckoning you on to something better? We can all ask ourselves the same question. I did many times. There are all kinds of reasons for this. For example, we are constantly bombarded by negativity from the media on a daily basis.

There are many negative images on television, newspaper, the radio, magazines and now the Internet. These external influences whether we like it or not, can deeply effect us and bring us to low level of outlook. They can, but only if we *let* them. If we give them permission to impact us. And yes being human we cannot be but moved deeply when we see images of war, famine, injustice and so on. What I am saying is not to subject yourself constantly to the media's ear. Give yourself a break perhaps for one, or two days or even a week. Try it. It works. So for us to be strong to allow our shift in positive thinking, we need to ask the question "Why?" Ask yourself "Why do I think like this?" Where does it come from? Where did I get this idea?" We must probe deeply to get the answers. When you know what your paradigm is on any given subject matter, create a positive affirmation that will help in the reprogramming of your mind. Something that is very positive, the opposite of your paradigm. Repeat these affirmations daily. Perhaps write them down, somewhere where you will be able to see them. Feel them. Incorporate them into your very essence. You will at first notice subtle more posive changes beginning to happen in your life. And over time with repetition, a new more positive YOU will start to emerge. Like the analogy I made earlier of the Caterpillar turning into the Butterfly. It had to undergo a *huge* transition. A long and arduous journey and it did not happen over night. Anything worthwhile rarely does. But in the end, you will emerge with a greater freedom, a totally new perspective on the world and its surroundings. I am not saying change who you are, but *in addition* to who you are, shake off the negative mindset which has left you stuck. Take on a new one. A fresh one. We are not Prisoners from our Past, but rather *Products* from the Past. This was one of my husband's favourite sayings. And I am now only beginning to live this philosophy. It WORKS! We have *choice* and only you can do it for yourself. No one else can. We must choose. And so began my Journey of Revelation. From here on in I will mainly relate the events and the synchronities which were to change my whole perceptive on reality and that around me. It both amazed and confounded me at the same time. I questioned my logic to what was beginning to happen around me. I started to delve more deeply into the spiritual world and did some research to further enlighten my mind to what it was that I was beginning to witness. I began to notice that alot of 'Spiritual Teachers' were coming into my life. Totally not of my doing. But they were presenting themselves to me via books, chance meetings, e mails, and any other avenue of connection one can think of. 'When the Student is ready – the *teacher* will appear'. This was a saying I had always liked but never fully understood the power and deep resonance of it until now.

For me back then I truly had thought my life was over. As I said before in a sense it was. I had to find a new one. I had no choice. I had two children to raise by myself. I was like the walking wounded. Life had lost its sparkle. It was grey inside and out. I could not see any light at the end of any tunnel. Even this metaphor the 'light' I was thinking of was an oncoming train hurdling at me at tremendous speed. I prayed for an escape to the misery I was in. Nothing seemed to change externally. But very subtly at first I began to perceive that a change was indeed happening within my being and my consciousness. I would like to share with you the following fascinating events which have brought me back on the road to recovery. The *self* I knew and thought I had lost forever was starting to show itself again.

Chapter 3

SYNCHRONICITY

Life's Circumstances does not make a man – it reveals Him.

I hope that by my sharing the following experiences, it will enlighten and question your own perspective on life and the possibilities of a life here after. We all have our own views on what we may or may not think happens to us after our own physical life ceases to exist. I was no different. I had always hoped and wanted to believe that we do go on in some order of existence better than this one we know to call life. I was starting to realize that something outside of my five senses was beginning to manifest itself. Logic and rationale went out the window so to speak. As I related before, when my daughter was a baby she *saw* something that evening which was meant only for her eyes. All I was able to do was to be a witness to her remarkable interaction with an unknown presence. As the years passed, although I never forgot what happened with her, I had somewhat basically put it to the back of my mind. Life just got in the way as they say. Our life was unfortunately plagued with more sadness and disappointment to come rapidly after loosing our first baby. I went on to have two more miscarriages. So in total, we had lost three babies in the early years of our marriage. The 'Why us' questions were hard to fathom. Each loss was as profound and as painful as the one which went before. But at least we did have one child and we were very grateful for that. It wasn't until six years later that a little boy was born into our family. He was beautiful. I realize that now. But after loosing three babies prior to having this baby we discovered that he was different but as special and as precious as any other baby was and we loved him dearly. He had special needs and I will admit back then my shock and disappointment in not having the 'perfect' baby hit me hard. But my husband had said and I thought it so eloquent back then that "He was a different kind of perfect." And he was right in saying so. We did not see what he could not do, but rather marvelled and celebrated in all that he *could* do. He was still our child, and we would not change him for the world. He is now one of my best friends and his smile and his laughter have lit up many lives with his wisdom, empathy, and love for others. I have and continue to learn from him every day.

I can now see the rich lessons which he has taught me and thus enabled my growth as a person to reach a higher level. And they do say that hindsight is a good thing. That with all the adversities which we have had in our life, they were actually paving the way for one of the biggest shocks I would encounter only three years later. All the other sadness could not hold a candle to loosing one's 'Soul Mate'. And this was exactly what happened to me. It was only shortly after my husband's passing that very unusual coincidences or synchronities started happening to me. A good friend had given me the book 'PS I Love You'. I had it for awhile and had intended to read it. But there always seemed to be jobs to do or activities with the children to attend. And one night, a few weeks after loosing my husband I decided to pick this book up and began reading it. It was also about a young widow so my interest was grabbed immediately. In the book, the character of the husband sends his wife several letters giving her a specific task to do which he hopes will make her stronger and happier after he is gone. At the end of each of the letters he says: *PS I LOVE YOU*. I really enjoyed this book but my sadness and apathy was beginning to impinge upon my own life. I could feel myself sinking further and further into the myre of depression. One night I asked Owen that if he was with me could he *please* give me a sign. Any sign no matter how small. I went into a deep fitful sleep after a few hours of twisting and turning. When I awoke, I went down the stairs and noticed a large brown envelope had been pushed underneath my door. This was unusual to begin with. I walked up the hall and pulled it out and there was nothing particular about it. When I opened it there was a beautiful printed Poem entitled "To My Dearest Family." It began by: -

*Some things I'd like to say but first of all to let you know that
I've arrived okay.*

I am writing this from heaven where I dwell with God above

*Where there are no more tears or sadness, there is just eternal
love*

Please do not be unhappy just because I am out of sight

Remember that I'm with you every morning noon and night.

And so it continued. A most beautiful rendition of something
someone close to us would say if they could who has passed on.
For the purpose of my explaining the co-incidence which was
to follow I will leave it just at the first verse. I will write the rest
at the end of the book. But suffice to say at the very conclusion
of this entire poem it ends by saying: *PS GOD SENDS YOU
HIS LOVE ....*

I could not believe my eyes. Only the previous night I had asked
Owen for a sign. And bearing in mind the title of the book I
was reading, well I think without question, I received my SIGN.

The first *synchronicity* had entered my life. And it was to be one
of many. The poem pushed under my door was sent by a lovely
girl, a parent at my daughter's school. She thought I would like
the sentiments and consoling words included in the poem. Little
did she know the huge ramifications it would have to me that
morning as I picked this large brown envelope up off the floor
and saw my first *sign.* As it so happened, at a later stage, I was
also given the same poem by a cousine of my husband. So I
really felt that this was substantiated quite strongly. I know
some people would perhaps dismiss this off as a coincidence
of sorts. But I just *knew* intrinsically that something was going
on here. I was not alone. He was still with me and the children.

Still guiding, still loving, still protecting. I must say in the early months I don't even know if I fully believed any of this. Well, I never had reason to do so as nothing profound on this topic had ever entered my life before. I merely thought it was my grief distorting the fabric of my reality and perhaps I was twisting events around to suit what I was *hoping* to be a sign. Later, I was without any doubt that there was more to this three dimensional world outside of our five senses. Something else was getting my attention but I was neither able to prove or disprove it efficiently. To explain it to myself never mind trying to talk about it with others. I will remember the first 'dream' I had after Owen died. It seemed so real. As did all the other 'dreams' that were to follow. In this dream, I found myself sitting up on the edge of my bed in my room. I looked towards my bedroom door and standing just inside the door was my husband. He was wearing a pale green jumper which he had worn in life. He appeared to be surrounded by a bright light. He stared at me for a little while tilting his head slightly to one side smiling and said: "Don't be sad." And with that he just faded. I remember waking up feeling very emotional. Happy, sad, confused and amazed all at once. It was SO real. So tangible. But then dreams are not tangible. We cannot grab their essence physically. They are a virtual projection of our subconscious mind.

I was not sure any more. But the visions and dreams I had which followed were not like your average common garden type variety. They were more colourful, more vivid, more detailed. I could *feel* my surroundings. I was able to participate and interact within the *dream*. Anyway I became fascinated with all things Spiritual. I needed to learn more. To explore. Why were we here. What is our purpose? And the biggest question of all "Where do we go to after we leave this mortal coil?"
I began watching programs that included subject matter with the paranormal. Mediumship intrigued me. I always had an interest in this area. But not until now did this interest become my search for answers. It was beckoning me like a beacon in the dark. There was one programme on television during the months

which followed my bereavement. It was the "Ghost Whisperer" the main character played by Jennifer Love Hewitt. I watched every episode. There was always a lovely message of hope in each story. This gave me great consolation. She portrayed a real person who could see people who had passed over to the Other Side. This intrigued me. I thought how wonderful to be able to have that ability. Some may not see it as a gift, perhaps even a burden which they may or may not be able to switch on or off. I began to notice as I watched this program I would get a tingling sensation like an mild electrical feeling around my body every single time I looked at it. This did not happen when I was looking at any other film or documentary etc. It only happened watching *this*. But it was not internal, it was *external*. Outside of myself and I just could not explain it. I must say that when I began to experience this physical sensation I would instantly think of and feel my husband's presence beside me. Invaribly I was nearly always alone when watching this. But I could not dismiss it either. It was real. Because we are unable to explain something, we should not dismiss it either. But I merely observed it. Sometimes it was stronger than at other times. But it was there. It was like some kind of force field around me. Like the feel of static electricity. This is the best way of describing it. But gentle not abrasive. Also something very reassuring about it. I just began to accept it after awhile. The next *dream* for want of a better word I had concerning my husband came a few weeks later.

In this dream I found myself sitting downstairs in my living room. My husband was sitting beside me wearing dark trousers, a white shirt, and black waist coat and tie. He wore this type of outfit alot when he was alive. He began to tell me in the dream "I would like you to go to America." I replied "No, it would not be the same without you." To which he replied "But I'll be with you." This incidentally was telepathic. I did not see his mouth move but we were having a conversation. With that, the door to my living room opened and these hazy figures started coming into the room. I realised in my dream that I could see them, but they seemed not to see me. I then said to

Owen "Look at these people, they cannot see me but I can see them. If only I could see you like the way I can see these figures, the rest of my life would be bearable." As soon as I said this, he leaned forward in his chair with his hands joined out in front of him and looked down at the floor. He never said another word, but I knew that it would not be possible for me to see him in this life dimension. His action alone confirmed this. And then the dream faded away. Looking back though this was what I wanted more than anything else. But I now know that my growth and my continued journey and mission in my life would not be able to progress the way it was meant to be if I was to see him constantly. He wanted me to move on with my life. But all I wanted was to be with him. It was not my time. I know that now. Following this I thought that maybe a trip to the states would be a good distraction. I would be away and out of my environment and hopefully begin to feel less claustrophobic. My grief was still strong. It was now eleven months since he died. I decided I would visit my sister with my daughter and try to heal my wounds. So after phoning her and arranging in a couple of weeks to visit I added that it would be wonderful to meet an authentic person who could talk to the 'other side.' "Leave it with me she said and I will get back to you on that." Not thinking much more about this I began planning my trip. In the meantime I began devouring books on the topic of the after life and reading about people connecting with their loved ones who had passed over. It was my solace. My retreat. One such book which I absolutely loved was "Talking To Heaven" written by a very gifted medium and beautiful human being called James Van Praagh. The moving and sensitively written depictions of people touched by the other side was both breadth taking and heart warming. I read and re read this so many times. Each time gleening a new lesson and perspective on this fascinating issue.

I began to have an Epiphany. I was definitely awakening to a different level of consciousness around me. I felt I was becoming part of something much bigger than myself. Something of which I could not fully explain. But it was happening. We can all have our hypothesis on the subject of the Afterlife. Some people dismiss it completely out of hand. What they cannot *see* must therefore not exist. But that is not the case. I always like to make the analogy of being in a room by oneself. It may appear we are alone. But there are electrical, eletromagnetic, and microwave energy to name but a few going through us, around us, below and above us. We cannot *see* this but it is real it just does not *appear* to be taking up any space around us. I like to equate this with Spiritual energy as well. Again because we are unable to see this energy those of us that is who do not have mediumship abilities, we should not say either that it does not exist. Most people are focused purely and only on literal linear thinking. In other words, what one can only see in front of them and nothing else. But life is so much more than that. This was what I was beginning to discover and discover more I did. It became empowering to me and like a beacon in the blackest of darkness, it beckoned to me and gave me courage and appreciation that we do go on after we leave this life. My husband showed me this on nearly twenty different occasions through the medium of dreams. I will not be able to recount every one of these *interactions,* but I will share some more with you in the coming chapters. If nothing else I really hope that it will give others who have lost someone very close to them, the consolation and knowledge that they do not leave us ever. We will see them again. They are around us. Guiding, helping, inspiring us. We only need to listen for the signs and wait for the answers.

Before my trip to the States back in the summer of 2007 I was keen to meet a gifted medium. I have heard so many stories of people being duped by others claiming to have this gift and leaving feeling distraught and utterly disappointed. But for me this was when the next incredible synchronity occured. My sister said that indeed she was put in touch with someone who had this wonderful talent. And bearing in mind that I had watched avidly my favourite programme for the first year after my husband died "Ghost Whisperer". The next thing I realise was that the person I was about to meet had very close connections with the show in Los Angeles. He was also the author of my *bible* 'Talking to Heaven' at that harrowing time in my life. I was to meet *James Van Praagh*. Even stranger, I had actually had a copy of his book in my hands while my sister was phoning me up to tell me the news. How amazing was that! Well, I just could not believe my luck. I was to meet this gentleman only two days later. I could barely contain my excitement. He was and still is a world famous medium who has written such empowering books helping people all over the globe to heal and embrace hope in its highest order. So I was going to meet *him*. I remember hearing a saying awhile back and it goes something like, *Life starts happening when you stop making plans* .. How true I found this to be. We can only orchestrate so much of our lives, but we are also governed by a higher force which will ultimately dictate the direction our lives will go. I used to say to myself when I first became a widow that all my dreams and plans for the future were now gone. Blown apart. I had made all these plans. But then I heard that God has a 'bigger and better plan' for each one of us. It may not appear like that particularly when terrible and sad events touch our lives. But we all have to hold true that in time we will see the bigger picture.

Chapter 4
NEW BEGINNINGS

When I arrived in California jet lagged and weary my heart was beginning to feel a little lighter. Leaving behind my routine was a welcome diversion. I needed new physical surroundings to help me work through so many questions I was having. Questions about the meaning of life. Why are we here? What is our purpose? I did not know the answers to any of these. But I needed to at least search and see if I could get any useful information. Initially I was taken up with the exciting meeting I was due to have the next day. I had all my books ready hoping to have them signed. The anticipation was all consuming. I felt like a little child about to get their best present ever. I was certainly about to get mine. The person who introduced James to my sister was a long time friend of hers. She in herself was such a joy to meet. Another beautiful soul who touched my life with gold dust. Sadly, she has since passed on but the short time we knew one another, there definitely emerged a warm friendship. Her name was Violette and like her name she was like a flower. So beautiful, real, and down to earth. But it was not to be my honour to have her long in my life as she did pass on not very long after meeting her. If I felt the loss hard I cannot imagine those who knew her for years the enormity of their grief must have been deep. She was just that kind of person. Sweet and giving. Eager to please. It was a priviledge to have met her. As I was saying, she introduced my sister and I to James Van Praagh that August back in 2007. It was a meeting that would change my life forever.

We were to meet him in Violette's house. She made me feel so welcome. The view from her living room was spectacular. I was staring out at this while she was busy making wonderful sandwiches and so on. I was a bundle of nerves. I did not know what to expect. What would I say? Would he be able to meet me? I did not want to impinge on his privacy. But I had doubts that he may not be able to meet me and I would have to accept this. Meeting Violette was a gift in itself. But yes I was to meet him. And he did appear. It was slightly surreal for me. Having all his books in my hands and meeting this person who had helped me so much and his connection with "Ghost Whisperer" was just too much to take in. He was charming and made me feel very much at ease. But I was in awe and a little shell shocked at first. "Would you like me to sign those for you?" he said pointing to the books. "Yes, that would be wonderful thank you" I said. I then told him about my husband's passing the summer before and how I got to hear about his books and was an avid viewer of "Ghost Whisperer." The next thing he said was like winning the Lotto even better. "I am going up to the set of "Ghost Whisperer" next week, would you like to come with me?" *Would I like to go ????* I just could not believe my luck. This wasn't happening to *me*. It must be a dream. It certainly felt so surreal the whole thing. But I knew it was *meant* to happen. I felt like the luckiest girl in the world. This was beyond my wildest dreams. It was just fantastic! I was going to go on the set and meet some of the actors – wow. Another synchronicity. No one could have planned something like this. Remember I said that life happens when we stop making plans? This was a testimony to the saying. And the rest is history.

We do not need to be defined by our circumstances. We can learn from the past. But the future can again be lived inch by inch without what happened before stifling our efforts to move forward in a *new* way. We will never forget what has shaped us all in who we are today as people. Yes, certain life events can have a more critical effect on how we choose to live our lives again. But with time and determination we will have the ammunition to create new goals and new horizons. Sometimes despite becoming stagnant by standing still for too long, a person or an incident can renew our faith in living. Never be afraid to ask for help. It is a sign of strength not weakness. We all have our own vunerbilities. Some more obvious than others. As human beings we need to reach out and allow friends or family to step in for a certain period and steer us to shore. Life is full of possibilities. Full of amazing and wonderous situations.

People want to be part of a bigger picture in their own lives and helping you to be one in yours. This was what I began to do with my life back then. I had lost all sense of direction and even purpose in my life. I still had two children to raise, but for myself I just had this huge void inside. Nothing could fill it. What gave me the strength quite early on was the possibility and more over, the probability that there is something much bigger to come after we die. And again there were so many spiritual teachers touching my life. This validated for me again that I was on the right path to discovery. When one truly feels excited about any type of venture, you know that you are on the correct journey for you. Sometimes there are sign posts along the way to guide us. But at other times we may loose clarity and motivation to proceed if we fall by the wayside. Despondency is a human condition we can all be prone to it at one time or another. Depending on your state of mind at any given time. Negative thinking can prevent us moving forward by creating a fog which makes planning for the future difficult. But it is transitory. It does pass. We need to mind ourselves, to cocoon ourselves during times of crisis. When I started doing this I found a new strength and resilience which helped me to overcome future obstacles. It was very difficult at first but over time I found that the darkness and the sorrow was starting to ebb. The person I once was began to change not leave. I was still me. But in addition to who I was, I was becoming a stronger individual. I had to do so much more things by myself which I never would have had to do if my husband was alive. You have to come out of your comfort zone in order to grow and expand. Expansion can happen in subtle and wonderous ways. With the passage of time eventually anything is possible. But it is so hard to see this when you are at the bottom of that proverbial pit. Here there is depression, hopelessness and apathy. All are rampant in that negative mind set. Apathy being the worse one. Just existing. Not really living. Functioning on a daily basis because you have to, not necessarily because you want to. I was in this robotic mode for years. Just existing. It was the epitomy of blandness. The complete opposite to how we are meant to live our lives. Until you are in this situation it is indeed very hard to empathise completely with people who have gone through any catastrophe. But just to listen is healing. Having gone through what I did, it seemed impossible to be enticed into any kind of advancement towards recovery. I was my own prisoner. My own jail keeper. My comfort zone became my retreat. It was the unknown that kept me isolated.

My dream came back to me with great resonance when my husband told me that he would like me to go to the States. He must have foreseen what was yet to come. I am told that when we cross over our consciousness becomes much more expansive then when we are here on earth. For example, take the following analogy. You are driving along a road and you will have a certain perspective in your field of vision.. But if you were in a small plane and you were moving over the same area the *perspective* of the landscape would be completely different. It is only the vantage point which has changed. The environment remains the same. But you would have the added benefit of seeing further, more clearly, and with much more detail and clarity then if you were at ground level. Also they can see a little further in time. How many times have you heard people been given warnings in dreams of a future event which has come true by a loved one who has passed. Time does not exist the same way it happens here. We have a past, present and future. Our time is man made. Dictated by days, weeks, months centuries and milleniums. But time in the after life is not measure by minutes or hours. There is just space. A continuum. It always was, is and always will be adfinitum. The concept of infinity is extremely hard to contemplate. Meeting James and going to the set of my favourite programme I have no doubt were all foreseen. A further validation that again I was being guided every step of the way. Then the communications kept on coming from him. Some short, some long. But he was still *with* me. I felt his presence so many times. My time in the States began to re invent everything about my life. It was a pivital turning point on my journey. And I was also fortunate to have made some great friendships from it. I had also lost my father a year before to the week that I lost Owen. A huge loss of two most fundamental men in my life within the year. Just two weeks before my husband died he had completed a very successful solo concert in piano. Before each piece of music, he would give a small verbal vinyette an evocative depiction of the music he was about to play. He would express how linked our lives were to the music and the sentiments of the composers. He played Bach, Haydn, Edvard Grieg, Chopin Claude Debussy and many more. It was always his life's dream to perform a solo piano recital and he did. He actually went out on his dream. He achieved all he wanted and needed to do. Although to me his young life was cut short at the height of his glory.

OWEN WALSH
Piano Recital

Painting the picture with sound

Programme

This was the programme used during Owen's recital in Airfield House

39

During this Recital I noticed that when he got up to speak to the audience he moved so many people who were present. One of the speeches he gave was before the 'Nocturnes' or *Night Pieces*. And I remember he started by speaking of a couple who were walking along a beach one night. It was a beautiful night. The sky was clear and you could see the stars and the full moon. They were alone walking hand in hand. Happy and in love. He said and I will quote "The following year there is only one of the couple walking alone along the same beach because their partner had died. But the one left behind had become a stronger and better person for having had their partner in their lives." He never said who had passed, the man or the woman. It did not matter at the time. But what seemed strange was a foreboding I was feeling when he said this. And I remember thinking to myself that I did not feel comfortable with him saying this. Even though there was no logic to feel this way. But I did. He began to play and many in the room that night were moved to tears. Young and old. Men and women. He had mentioned at the beginning how we had both met and how his life had unfolded. Looking back it wasn't just his depiction and expression of the music, he was also telling his life story even to the last piece. And two weeks later he was dead. It was like he *knew* he was not going to be in this world for much longer. It was I who was half of the couple left. I who did become a much stronger person for having had him in my life. Everyone present who knew him all agreed that he was *saying goodbye*. He was painting the pictures of his life with the music of the Greats. I used to think that we were people *with* Souls. But the truth of the matter is that we are *Souls having a human experience*. And not the other way around. When we think about this for a moment it does change our perspective on life and how we view each other. We are all connected. We all come from the same place and will return to the same place but on different levels. Depending on our time here in the class room of life will dictate how far our soul evolves and what level we go to next. I also believe that each one of us has been given a job to do here. Sometimes it is not made very clear to us. We might stumble along the way and encounter obstacles. If we are on the right path things appear to go much smoother. I have found this. Destiny is trying to tell you something when you come up against blocks and disorder. Are you where you should be? Are you on the right path? Some find it sooner than others. There will be the sign posts along the way. We can accept them or ignore them.

My husband always wanted me to write. I said perhaps. Some day maybe. But I never fully knew what it was that I wanted to write about. It was only through my personal catastrophe of loosing my husband and with the passage of time that I got the epiphany to write this book. I felt such a *strong* pull from the other side to write of my Spiritual experiences and being *touched* by the Light. I sincerely hope that by my doing so now it will help others. Even one person who gets a glimmer of hope that there is more to this world than meets our eyes. There is so much more Spiritual awareness around the world. Now more than ever. People are searching for answers. We need to know more.

The answers are more likely to happen. Seemingly we here on this earth dimension are at a lower vibration compared to those in Spirit. They are at a higher vibration or frequency. But when we are asleep we are at a higher level, a raised frequency. And they can lower their vibration and the *window* in between the two states is where they can communicate with us. And the way they can do this more effectively is through our dreams. When we are clouded in sadness and grief it is harder for them to make contact with us. I was amazed only a few weeks after my husband passed that the first dream was able to get through to me. There must have been such denseness around my aura that it would have been very difficult for any connection to have been successfully achieved. But they are tenacious and so was my husband in life. Anything he ever wanted and focussed on he got through hard work and determination. And they don't change when they move on. We can learn to listen more effectively through meditation. It is sometimes hard to get a few moments to yourself throughout the day to try and take time out for this. And to let ones mind go blank in of itself is a very difficult state to reach. I would love to be able to meditate more successfully. I am told over time and with practice the technique will improve.

Our minds can meander and 'junk' can just flow in and distract our focus.

Owen was constantly encouraging his students to fulfil their highest potential in both the musical field and in the area of their personal growth and self esteem. Here was one of many concerts he gave which he would show case the abilities of his 'Musical Family'. He was indeed the 'Mr. Chips' of the Music World and loved dearly by students and parents alike.

There are so many books written about meditation. Some better than others. One way I was told as well as guided visualizations is to clear your mind and simply 'listen'. Turn off mobile phones, televisions, radios, any external noise pollution if possible and go into the most quiet space in your home. To choose an environment which is devoid of distractions is a good start. Begin with fifteen minutes to start developing mental and physical focus. Maintain a comfortable but upright posture. And be aware of the temperature that it is not too hot or cold. Breath deeply in through the nose and out through the mouth. Try to form a natural rhythm with your breathing. You will notice over time that it will begin to slow as the process of relaxation gets deeper. Bring your full attention onto your breath. Take note of the pauses between your breathing. Some people find lighting a candle good and just staring at the flame can focus our attention a little easier. We will all have our own methods of achieving this. Some of you may prefer to have music in the background. Others to have silence. Whichever works for you is the correct one to have. Try to meditate once per day. For short periods at a time in the beginning. Choosing what time in the day or evening will have to fit in with your own schedule. But be consistent. The evening time is good to wind down from the day. Or the morning to prepare for the day ahead. One's state of mind is important. Having a calm mind will make for a more successful outcome during meditation. So avoid meditating directly after a stressful day or event.

There are so many good reasons to meditate. As well as an aid to help with relaxation it also increases brain function and helps to eliminate stress. You will know you are being successful at meditation when you are aware of your thoughts and not being controlled by them. Transcendental Meditation refers to a specific form of mantra meditation called Transcendental Meditation technique. The transcendental meditation and transcendental Movement were introduced in India in the mid 1950s by Maharishi Mahesh Yogi (1918-2008). The TM technique involves the use of a sound or mantra and is practiced for fifteen to twenty minutes twice per day. It is said to be a means of relaxation and stress reduction. It is one of the most widely practiced, and among the most widely researched meditation techniques. TM is taught in a standardized, seven-step course over a four day period by certified teachers. It is up to you which area of relaxation is the most effective. And when you find out what that is, to try and stay with it and let it become an efficient tool to strengthen your ability to unwind and recharge your mind and body.

Investing a small amount of time for your overall well being will be the best investment you will make. And also your family and friends will all equally benefit from a more revitalised and peaceful you.

"We tend to think of meditation in only one way,
But life itself is a meditation."
- Raul Julia.

Chapter 5

REVEALATIONS

Imagination is everything, it is a preview of life's coming attractions.

There was one particular dream which was like no other I have had before or since my husband's passing. I had just got the two children off to school and I had not slept much the previous night. It was a bleak and cold winter's morning outside and I decided I would have a rest for just an hour to recharge my batteries. At this time I was both physically and emotionally depleted of energy. I remember lying there thinking of all the jobs that needed to be done and before I knew it I fell into a deep sleep. I say *deep* but yet it was somewhat lucid in so far as I could feel the couch beneath me and was aware of my body. However, I started *dreaming* I was outside this particular room and at the entrance of this room was a hazy shadowy figure I think male sitting down. I remember looking into this room and noting that it was a very long and dark room with some sort of long desk in the middle.

Behind this desk at the end of the room was a man who looked extremely like my husband. I was thinking this to myself and then the figure at the entrance began talking to me about my daughter and how well she was doing. "You are not listening to me" he said. "Sorry I think I know the person in that room I don't mean to be rude." And with that I was slowly propelled into the room and wanting so much to go to the person who looked so like Owen. Even within this dream I was saying to myself something to the effect of, "As soon as I get closer to this person he will look nothing like him." But the opposite happened.

Now bear in mind that this was all in my dream, but it was incredibly detailed and real. When I got close to him I found myself behind this *desk* or boundary of sorts and was looking up from my side at him. It was my husband clear as day. He did seem to notice me at the beginning but appeared to be busying himself with something which I could not see. I began calling his name several times. On the third time I called his name I got his attention and he looked down at me. He was wearing a navy suit with a white shirt and a navy tie. He had owned this suit when he was alive and had called it 'his lucky suit'. He simple said "Good Morning Phyllis." Nothing profound, no complex message, nothing unusual. Just a greeting and it *was* time appropriate. It was 9.00am in the morning in my reality. He then gave me the most brilliant smile . I wanted to get closer but there was this division between us and he was on his side, and I was on mine. I suppose it was the barrier between the two dimensions the two worlds. What we know as this life, and the hereafter. I really do not know. This was my speculation. But then something happened next which I will never forget. Just when he greeted me a door or some kind of opening from behind me gave way to a beautiful gold light. He just looked beyond me gazing with wonder at this light. I did not take my eyes off him. I could not move. I remember seeing this gold light illuminate the left side of his face very brightly. And with that this beautiful light expanded around him and he began moving up higher and higher above me into it. It was as if it was beckoning him. As if he was given this special time to connect briefly with me and say hello. I could feel my disappointment as I was thinking saying "Oh no, I am loosing the connection." And as swiftly and as immediate as my dream began it was over in an instant. I cannot recall in human terms how long the time frame of this was. It could have been second or minutes. It seemed for *hours* but I *know* we were together for some duration whatever it was to let me know that he was fine and doing well. What was remarkable about this dream for me unlike any other dream before, was the interchange of dialogue and the detail of everything. But bearing in mind also that I could still *feel* the couch beneath me physically, but although my *body* was there, *I* was somewhere else. I had definitely gone somewhere outside of the five senses which I was not familiar and had no knowledge of. Perhaps a type of astral projection. I do not know. Since we cannot experience bilocation. It is just not possible to be in two places at the same time. Because physically I was in my living room. But there must have been some astral projection occuring simultaneously into another time frame another environment. This I had never experienced before. I was so keen to tell people close to me what had occured that morning. I know some might have put this down to grief or exhaustion. No matter what one may feel or think, I *know* what happened to me was *not* a dream. Yes, the dream state was used to facilitate this encounter. But yet it was *not* a dream. I went somewhere. Perhaps a waiting area of sorts between the living and the deceased which can allow for the briefest of times, a connection between us to let us know that although their earthly bodies have ceased to exist, they do indeed continue to live on in another dimension. They *are* o.k. This can be so reassuring to those of us who are left behind to pick up the pieces after and during a bereavement. It is their way of helping us along the journey of grief into one of acceptance and finally peace. It can be a very long and difficult journey for some. For others perhaps with different coping mechanisms they may not find it as painful. We all have our own tools to cope in the face of adversity. Mine was to become a spiritual tool due to the several communicatons I have had since loosing my loved one over recent years. Some psychics say that the subconscious or dreaming mind contains the spirit or astral body, resulting in falling dreams or waking up with a falling sensation or sudden jerk. We do dream every night but most of our dreams are not remembered by the conscious mind. Etheric Projection in contrast to Astral Projection involves the traveler moving about in usually invisible or ghost like form. Mental projection is projection of the astral body to the mental plane through the utilisation of mental energy. While within the astral to phase into the Mental Plane. The active subtle body of the mental plane is the mental body which makes up the intellectual consciousness of the projector. The environment is usually very colourful and kaleidoscopic in nature.

Medieval civilizations, hindus and spirtual leaders have documented the theory of astral projection or out of body experiences. (OBE). The theory that it is possible for a person to leave the physical body and experience something beyond the physical realm. Perhaps this was what was happening to me at that time. The spiritual explanation of astral projection for some people gives them spiritual clarity. Their intuition is enhanced. And they have a greater understanding and appreciation of people around them. Also a better understanding of their circumstances. I am not the only one to experience this type of dream which I had where I *met* my husband. Others have also experienced hyper-realistic dreams which allows them to project their consciousness to another location. The belief that we all possess an astral body. That it is connected to the physical body through the umbilicus (the navel) along what is known as the silver cord. And it is this cord which is severed when we die. Astral projection can also be triggered through both meditation and hypnosis. The symptoms are quite like that of an out of body experience. One experiences the physical world from an etheral perspective which is being able to float through doors, walls or any solid object.

We all need hope and to be hopeful. Depending on our belief systems and what support we have around us can all impact both positively and negatively. And it was not just my husband who made contact with me since he left. I had also lost my father who died the year before to the week that I lost my husband. And I remember the following summer I was unsure whether or not to take my four year old on the transatlantic journey or leave him with my mother in law Kitty here at home. Shortly afterwards, I had a dream about my father and in it he was sitting down with his legs crossed out in front of him. His arms were folded across his chest and the sleeves on his shirt were rolled up to his elbows. He asked me what I was pondering over and I told him. Should I bring my son with me to the States or leave him behind"? And his reply was as follows "Look if Kitty said she will look after him well then I would leave him with her, after all she will take very good care of him." And that was it. I had my answer loud and clear. I woke up the next morning *knowing* the right thing to do. I had been given my answer. Kitty is my children's grandmother, and she was such a help and rock to us all and still is. After all she lost a son and that must be the most horrific of losses to loose a child.

They say if you loose a spouse you loose your past, but to loose a child you loose your future. All losses are relative. All different. All lessons. All hard, but death is so much *part* of life. It is a natural process. But we as a society do not like to talk about it. We rather use euphonisms and gently sweep the topic away in hushed tones. In time we can celebrate the person who is no longer with us. We can laugh at the funny times, the warm times, embrace their memories and still feel at a deeper level that they have not left us completely just physically. And yes this is the part which is the hardest to accept. The empty chair the silence. All tangible reminders that they are no longer there. And the familiar is not available to us anymore. We have to learn to adapt to settle for a different life. A new one. It does not have to end. It merely *changes*. But change can be tough. We are very resilient as human beings. We have to accept our new reality. We do not have to like it . But we have to adapt. Circumstances change. Change is inevitable. Like the changes of the seasons, night following day. And as people we can encounter change in our everyday life. Change can be a useful tool. We can turn our situations around. We can grow and expand and become stronger in the process. It takes time. Sometimes we find that the change can be internal. At times it has to be internal for us to survive and continue to have a fundamental participation in life. And this can take a long time. I know. I am one of those people. I locked myself away into my comfort zone for years. Initially, I was not able to do anything else. But with the passage of time and life pulling me along with it despite my reluctance, I did emerge out the other side stronger and with a deeper understanding of myself. I certainly do not have the answers to everything. But with patience and discovery we are shown the answers in unusual ways. For me as I said I was touched by the other side. It was an intrinsic lesson of discovery. And it began to resound strongly. But I loved the consolation I received from it. I began to embrace it. Not to be frightened by it. But merely to accept, even if I did not fully understand it. But then I just knew that I did not have to. We do not have to fully understand everything in life in order to appreciate something. There are on occasions incidents which happen to us which make us become observers. In other words, an incident which directly effects us and defys logic. The mind takes on this experience but our intellect will try to reject its existence. We are not *meant* to understand everything which happens around us. But what the inexplicable does is to raise our level of consciousness in order to try and explain it.

Around this time and up to the present, besides having these wonderful dreams, I also experienced unusual little things happening around me. For example I would be looking at the television when all of a sudden the channel would change by itself. I would have dismissed this if it happened just once or twice, but it has happened several times and on difference television sets. So I did not have the excuse that there was something faulty wrong with one specific television. Also lights flickering on and off by themselves. It is not unusual for electronics to experience faults which can cause them to do unusual malfunctional episodes. This has not only happened in my own house but in other people's homes. Sometimes I am alone and other times I am with people. This is another way we can have communication from those who have passed over. They are able to manipulate electrical appliances. Because we are all energy. And energy can never be distroyed only changed. I have also had my alarm system go off and it was not even switched on! I called out the engineer to check the system was working and he could not find a fault. Daunting though this may be for some I was never disconcerted or worried when any of this happened. Instead I became an observer without having prejudice either way. To have an open mind is important. It humbles our intellect without curtailing it. I also believe that we will get the signs for which we are open and ready for. Some may be intimidated by anything paranormal and would prefere for nothing to happen. While others are so eager to glimpse a sign, any sign where they could identify a connection. We are all different and that is fine. There is always a certain degree of a fear factor when we are unable to explain the inexplicable. But instead of shying away from the unknown we should start to question and expand our knowledge to what may be happening. To start to think outside of the box and not be defined by paradigms. Out moded and rigid thinking just shuts us down.

Pictures falling off walls. Furniture being arranged or moved I have also experienced. But only one time. For me looking back, there was one phenomenon which happened quite regularly which was my son's powered toys switching on by themselves. And the sense that I could feel a gentle touch usually on my face or back. But again I never felt afraid only a sense of a loving presence. A reassurance. Like having a companion just drop by to see how you are. There was never a feeling of foreboding or fear. As I have become stronger as a person these activities have become less prevalent. There were other times when I would walk into a room and the scent of roses would be very strong. I could never see the origin of the scent. Sometimes it would be in a corner of the room and at other times the whole room would be filled with the aroma. And I would leave the room to return only moments later and there would be no remnants of the scent. And there was no logical explanation for this. But it has happened on several occasions. Unexplained noises at the beginning were also common. Not so much now. The sound of something being moved around a room. All signs and equally interesting in their nature.

I have included some thought provoking quotes below from the wisest of the great thinkers on the subject of death and the hereafter........

"Death may be the greatest of all human blessings." - Socrates

"The soul of man is immortal and imperishable." - Plato

"The immortality of the soul is demonstrated by many proofs." - Plato

"Death is simply a shedding of the physical body like the butterfly shedding its cocoon. It is a transition to a higher state of consciousness where you continue to perceive, to understand, to laugh, and to be able to grow." - Elizabeth Kubler-Ross

"There is not a grain of dust, not an atom that can become nothing, yet man believes that death is the annihilation of his being." - Socrates

"Do not expect to arrive at certainty in every subject which you pursue. There are a hundred things wherein we mortals ... must be content with probability, where our best light and reasoning will reach no further." - Isaac Watts

"Whatsoever that be within us that feels, thinks, desires, and animates is something celestial and divine and consequently imperishable." - Aristotle

"The important thing is not to stop questioning. Curiosity has its own reason for existing. One cannot help but be in awe when he contemplates the mysteries of eternity, of life, of the marvellous structure of reality. It is enough if one tries merely to comprehend a little of this mystery every day. Never lose a holy curiosity." - Albert Einstein

Chapter 6

LOVE FROM BEYOND

Life is not measured by the number of breaths you take, but by each moment that takes your breath away.
Anonymous.

My life was starting to be taken over by everything Spiritual. I felt it was my salvation at that time. I was not consumed by it but it was becoming a strong component in my life. It was subtle but constant. I noticed more and more unusual occurrences happening to me. One particular one stands out which touched me about four and a half years ago. It was October 2007. I had been staying with my mother for the evening and was returning to my home late that night. Again this was one of the many times I was feeling sorry for myself. Despondency seemed to be my kindred friend. However, as I was saying. This particular night I phoned for a cab to go home. I began to gather my belongings. I was going in and out from the front of the house to see when the cab would arrive. I remember having to go back into the kitchen to get something. When I went looking again there was the car waiting outside the gate. I told my daughter to take her little brother out while I said goodnight to my mother. When I was walking out of the house, the taxi driver a very good looking man had my little son on his lap and he had him sitting up with his little hands gripping the stearing wheel and turning it around as if he was driving. My son seemed delighted and there was a very happy interchange between the two of them. I heard him say "You are a great little chap and isn't this fun pretending to drive this car." My daughter sat in the front and I had got into the back of the car. I was glad of the darkness as I did not feel much like talking. I just wanted to get home and curl up inside. But instead of moving off and asking me where I wanted to go, he began talking to the three of us. He asked me about my son and where he goes to school, what age he was and so forth. Then he asked my daughter what school she was in. She began to tell him that she was going into a new high school and she was very nervous about making the transition and being the 'new girl'. "Don't worry" he said. There will be alot of other new girls there too. You will not be the only one and in time you will settle down and adapt nicely. You will be just fine". And I had mentioned from the back of the car that my husband had only died recently and it was difficult not having him around for big events with the children. He then turned to me and said looking me very directly in the face "Your husband is still parenting *very close by* but just in a different way. So please don't worry." He had lovely eyes even though it was dark and he was just so *nice*. I was hoping he did not see my tears but looking back it did not matter. I thought it was a lovely thing to say and a lovely perspective on which to think about my husband. We then belted up and began heading home.

When we arrived at my house, I thanked him for his words of encouragement and kindness and asked him how much I owed him. "Oh there is no charge for this don't worry about it." I told him that I could not accept this and I would feel embarrised if I ever met him again and not having paid him. "No you will never see me again just accept it." Well, I hope I do see you as you are so kind and not to charge me for the journey. I will not forget your kindness. Something about this situation deeply moved me and I was overcome with emotion. He gave me a big hug and said "Everything is going to be alright." With that he got back into the car and gave us all a really big wave and off he went into the night. That was four and a half years ago and yes I have never seen him again. And I have used that same company many many times. I even gave his description as best as I could to his colleagues and they could not decipher who he was from my description. But he was *different*. Who knows. I do believe in human angels. I also believe in the mysterious. Some incidents we encounter no matter how fleeting can effect us for years. I think that was one of those encounters I will remember as being quite unusual and very touching. The wisdom he imparted to the three of us was both simple and profound. His timing was second to none. I do believe that people come into our lives for a particular reason. It may be for a moment or for a lifetime and everything else in between. But they are there to either teach us something about ourselves or to teach us a lesson for our personal growth. We in turn can without our knowing effect so many other people for the better too. We can touch others in integral ways. Ways we may never be even aware of. But we *are* here for a reason. Let us find out what that reason is. Some are able to acknowledge this easier than others, but in time it will be revealed to us. Being purposeful can be good. Even perhaps not knowing what that purpose may be. If we are receptive to guidance it will be easier for us to establish our destiny. We need to listen. Listen internally as well as trying to get the external guidelines. *Something* was happening and it had got my attention. I was eager to learn more and learn more I did.

While doing some research on the Afterlife with my personal experiences still very fresh I came across a fantastic and informative site about the subject in all its glory. Anyone who is also interested should check this out. It is called Victor J. Zammit's AfterLife Report. 'A Lawyer presents the Case for the Afterlife.' A very appropriate title don't you agree. This gentleman has been exaiming the afterlife for the last twenty years. One of the topics which always held a fascination for me was the area of near death experience. I had never had one myself or for that matter met anyone who had. But none the less it was a fascinating subject concerning the next life if these cases were to be substanciated. It has been shown that following cases of NDEs that they have nothing to do with the brain lacking oxygen. It is not the result of a dying brain. Because then everyone would experience it if they were dying. This does not happen in every case. But these people were able to observe situations outside of the environment of their physical bodies at the time they were announced as being physically dead. So this would then put forward the argument that the brain is not the 'Creator of our consciousness', but rather the *facilitator* of it. In some cases there were blind people who were even able to *see* who was operating on them and around them. All of these people who came back from these experiences all became more Spiritual. They lost their fear of death and their appreciation for life and people grew more profound and deeper. They also became increasingly less materialistic and more gentle. Their perspective on life changed. There was one case where Victor relates the story of a lady called Pam Reynolds. She had undergone brain surgery. They had drained the blood from her brain for one hour and her ECG was flattened. Her heart was stopped and so was her breathing. Taking all of these important factors into account she still had an amazing NDE. She *saw* who was operating on her. She was also able to hear and see the nurses talking to the brain surgeon and hearing him give out his instructions to his other assistants. She went through the tunnel, a world wide reported phenomenon of NDEs. She saw the bright light at the end of this and had met loved ones she had lost before. This case shows us therefore that it is possible to have a Near Death Experience when the brain is absolutely dead. So are NDEs evidence of the After Life? We would have to conclude that there is a very high probability that they are. I had never met anyone who had experienced one of these. Yes, like a lot of people I had seen documentaries and read articles on the subject. But not until four months ago had I actually met someone who had gone through this phenomenon themselves. Strangely enough, at the time I was talking to this person I did not even remotely know I was going to write a book never mind on which topic. Again he was another cab driver I would say in his late fifties early sixties. We began talking about life and how valuable it was to have this gift. When he told me that fifteen years before he had a heart attack and had 'died' for a short period. I began next asking him "Did you happen to have a near death experience by any chance?" "Well I have rarely spoken about this but yes I did have one now that you ask," he said. Luckily for me I was working as a security guard and was on the grounds of a hospital when I remember walking towards a door and just collapsing. I was after having a heart attack and was in cardiac arrest.

After that I found myself in a beautiful meadow. As far as my eyes could see it went on forever. Trees, flowers, beauty beyond measure and the grass was so green. Everything was incredibly vivid and real. My surroundings and my senses were also super heightened. I could *feel* the grass beneath me. I could *smell* the flowers. Then I approached this little bridge. I will just have to add here that I had a complete distain for eggs during my life on earth. I could barely look at one without feeling nauseous. But in my NDE I had to consume an egg in order to get over this bridge to the other side. On the other side of the bridge was a nephew of mine who had died. My wife and I did not have any children of our own. So really my nephew was the closest person I had to having a child of my own and I loved him dearly. But as I was saying I had to put this egg into my mouth in order to meet my nephew who was waiting across the bridge. In my altered state I remember eating the egg and having a wonderous reunion with my young nephew. He looked so radiant and so happy to see me but had told me that it was not my time. I would have to go back. After this I do not remember anything else. I was unconscious for the best part of a week. But my wife who was at my bedside all the time heard me talking about an egg and the hearing me say the name of my nephew. This made absolutely no sense to her and she thought it was the ramblings of a confused mind. I had clinically *died* and was later resuscitated. Apparently when I came around I was told that my heart had indeed stopped for several minutes and they had 'lost' me. The bridge I felt represented the crossing over between this world and the next. A symbolism if you like. And for me to get back I had to do something which I really felt a discomfort for and that was to eat this egg. The 'egg' was probably something unpleasant for me to face in order to be reunited with my nephew. I do not know the answer. But I also wanted so very much to reach him in my altered reality. When I recovered and came out of hospital, I changed the group of people I had interacted with. They were boisterous and very materialistic. I left my job and became more appreciative of the simple things in life and I can tell you one main thing from all of this, I have absolutely no fear of death. It felt very peaceful and calm. I did not want to come back. I loved my wife dearly but where I went to was so incredibly beautiful that I desperately wanted to stay. I held on to this disappointment for several months to follow but it did awaken something deep within me. I became a better person. Less judgemental and more accepting of life and why I was here."

I told him that it was an absolute privilege to have met someone who had experienced this wonderful enlightenment and who was able to come through their ordeal and stand witness to the fact that they were a survivor and did live on to tell what happened. I told him about my loss and how I found the subject to be immensely fascinating and consoling. And there was one particular book I was trying to tell him to get but for the life of me I was unable to remember the title. I kept on saying the word *Beyond beyond* and unbeknown to me it was to be one of the words in two subtitles of this book I was to write shortly afterwards. That was no coincidence. Another synchronicity. I later thought back to our conversation and while I was pondering on one of titles for the book I remembered that word. I felt a strong compulsion to have it in the title even though I did not have the full idea of what to write on the cover. But I felt a guidance. A higher power if you like guiding me to this moment. I just had to get my experiences down on paper. If nothing else it was therapeutic to see what occurred by tangibly writing it down. A bonus to share it and a privilege if it helps even one person through the rough journey of loss. I really felt I was onto something great here. And I wanted and needed to share it with anyone willing to listen. I said to the taxi driver that his purpose here on earth was obviously not complete that he still had a mission to accomplish otherwise he would not be here talking to me. "I hope so," he said. We wished one another good luck with our prospective lives and parted ways.

But it was an enriching meeting and one I feel was truly meant to happen. I would like to believe he got something useful and insightful from our talk and interchange as well. Such is life. Strangers come in and out of our lives all the time. Everyone can teach us a lesson and we too can teach others.

I love the following poem and the soothing words when we think of those we have lost who are no longer with us. There is a strong consolation and dept of feeling that empowers us just a little. It is nice to take it out and absorb the sentiments when we are lonely and missing their physical presence.

"Death is nothing at all,
I have only slipped away into the next room,
I am I and you are you;
Whatever we were to each other, That we still are.
Call me by my old familiar name,
Speak to me in the easy way which you always used,
Put no difference in your tone,
Wear no forced air of solemnity or sorrow.
Laugh as we always laughed at the little jokes we shared together.
Let my name ever be the household word that it always was.
Let it be spoken without effect, without the trace of a shadow
on it.
Life means all that it ever meant,
It is the same as it ever was, there is unbroken continuity.
Why should I be out of mind because I am out of sight?
I am waiting for you, for an interval, somewhere very near,
just around the corner.
All is well."

-Henry Scott Holland
Canon of St. Paul's Cathedral, London

Chapter 7
FAITH AND EVIDENCE

Also around the time while writing this book I started attending a group which catered for widowed, separated, and divorced people. I certainly was not strong enough to be part of such a group even a year ago. But I felt a calling to be part of others lives who had shared a similar experience to my own. It was on the second attendance which again I had an interesting signal from my husband. For most of the duration of this session I felt his presence very strongly beside me. Again mentioning this tingling sensation I used to get shortly after he passed. I thought no more of it. But interestingly enough, on the way home on the radio a song began to play which I had not heard being played in my company that is in nearly seventeen years. It was the song "ON THE WINGS OF LOVE" sung by Jeffrey Osbourne from 1982. There are so many versions of this song but it was this exact one which was playing all the way home. I thought this very strange and had remarked to the person with me. The reason being that this particular song was the exact version chosen by my husband for our Wedding Video all those years ago... Now if that was not a message or what, I do not know what is. Some may brush it off as just another 'co-incidence' of sorts and say no more. But it did not end there. When I returned home my daughter was watching a film and she had asked me to have a look at it with her for a few minutes. And lo and behold in the background was another song being sung by Charles Aznavour called "SHE". This was yet *another* song which my husband had chosen for our Wedding Video back in 1994. And also like the above song there are other versions of the song 'She' but it was this version also we had played back then. One had to think this was just a *little* more then a *coincidence?* Two songs in the one night. Incidentally the two main characters in the movie my daughter said reminded her of her father and myself. Powerful. Another *Synchronicity.*

These signs are all around us we merely have to listen for their voice. We need to be more open I feel that is all. In time and at the right time we will get them and become empowered by them. Getting a sense that we are on the right path in our lives.

I knew then that the spirit of my husband was very much with me that night at my class and I found great strength and consolation to strive on with a more positive countenance. He wanted *me* I felt to help other people and spread my knowledge on the subject. Being human we use all the five senses. But the sixth sense the most mysterious and intangible of the senses really is the most intriguing of all. You know the feeling. You walk into a room, a house, a building, and there is just an *atmosphere* you pick up. It can be good, bad, or even omnimous. If we are indifferent to any sensation around us beyond the five senses, we pay no heed and continue on our way. But at times, we do need to pay attention. Everything is energy. Thought is energy. You cannot touch or feel it but it is there. Very real. It is the same when we meet people for the first time. Some people you are going to feel an empathy for even a bond of friendship when meeting them for the first time. Other people you may not feel very comfortable with. The *energy* is different. It is there between you. And we are *sensing* it. We should pay more attention to it. I never depend on first impressions. I have been proved wrong on so many occasions. We have to get to *know* the person but some are easier to do this with then others. We all put up certain barriers when we meet people for the first time. It can be a self protection mechanism. We want to give a good impression of ourselves. This is all perfectly natural and normal. But judging people out of hand by only a few initial moments can be inappropriate and unfortunate. Everyone should get a second or third chance, or for as long as it takes. Sometimes we can be having a bad day. Perhaps we heard some distressing news beforehand which can put us not in our best light. When we become ourselves we become more open to others, they usually in turn will begin to feel more relaxed and comfortable. They will as a result be able to be themselves. Empathy is a wonderful common denominator for breaking the ice with new people. If we can relate with others who have something in common with us, we can therefore share and exchange what we know. Having a common ground is an added bonus. When we are going through difficult life events like bereavement we have to be protective of our feelings. They are raw and shattered. We can become more defensive. Patience is the key to being more understanding to those bereaved. They are not that strong to put themselves out there in the public domain. It is a timely process and takes a different length and journey for every individual. But being more open to more then people. For example to our environment. To the unseen. To silence. It is sometimes in the silence that we can receive communication from loved ones who have crossed over. As I said I do not have any gifts in relation to being a medium or such a related skill. I am intuitive and a little psychic but then I believe everyone is psychic to one degree or another. This can be developed. But with my own connection to the other side it was always through dreams and especially the most real type like lucid dreams.

Lucid dreams being that one knows they are dreaming but can interact with the people and events within these dreams. Also the other signs like when I heard the two songs on the same night which were chosen years beforehand on our wedding video. I had never heard even *one* of them being played in my company since I got married on the radio like that. But to have the two of them on the same night and feeling the presence of my husband earlier on in the evening was enough to get my continued attention. And they were both nearly thirty years old. So they were not 'current' songs of the time. Our loved ones will try to connect with us every way they possibly can. They will use the radio, television, media, dreams and so forth to get us to know they are around and watching over us. I find this tremendously reassuring and consoling. Don't you? Meditation can also help with connecting. It is not an easy task. We are constantly bombarded with external noise all around us all of the time. To try and tune out all sound and listen to silence can be very difficult and to some slightly disconcerting. A hard task for many of us. I never minded the *sound* of silence. I know it is a paradox to say but it can be oppressive if you are not used to sitting still with no distractions. Silence can be *loud*. To focus only on your own breathing. The mind wanders. We start to think of what we should be doing. What needs to be done. Will this work? Will I get anything out of it? Different thoughts may come in and out of your mind. Just let them. If they are negative say "Stop It!" They have no control over you. But you have the control over what you permit to enter or not into your conscious mind. With practice this can be a very effective tool in becoming more receptive to the other side. We just have to try and keep some space for ourselves some quiet time throughout the day which we can be still and call our own. Find out what works best for you.

In life we do the best we can and we have our hopes, dreams and goals for the future. For the lucky few some of those dreams do come true. But for others no matter how much planning, preparation and hard work they take on, their goals never quite reach their reality. I have found that if you are on the right path in life eventually what you aim for will materialize. However there are occasions where your path may lead you down into an area say a career or a relationship which originally may not have been on your horizon. The saying '*What is meant for you will not pass you by...*' I have found this to be true. And also projects or events seem to follow the same principle. However again we are guided. And what I am about to relate will prove this point.

Because my husband was a well respected and much loved music teacher his family and particularly his mother thought it would be a lovely idea to have a small memorial stone placed discretely within the vicinity where he taught music. She proceeded to have this work carried out and within a relatively short space of time the stone was ready to be installed. There was a small mountain Ash tree planted over the stone and wonderful flowers were placed around the base to finish everything off. There was a small gathering of friends, family and neighbours along with a priest who said a few prayers and some nice words of remembrance. All went well for a couple of months to follow. As I mentioned before it was inobtrusive and extremely discreet. So much so that you would more likely miss this unless someone brought it to your attention. The reason why I mention this aspect was that secretly I would have liked it to be more prominent so more people could see this when they passed by. But because of planning laws and so forth it could only be placed where it was. However, there was an objection to the stone by someone who very quickly made an argument for the full removal of the stone and small plaque. We were all very saddened at this objection and so too were the neighbours who from the initial stages welcomed its arrival. And this is where my earlier point before about us sometimes being lead onto a different path in our lives. Or situations just not appearing to work out in our favour. We are not always in control with the planning and expectations we encounter. Owen's mother was naturally very saddened after all her hard work and patient planning to then have her son's memorial stone taken up and stored in her back garden where nobody could see it. Owen had attended his local school Benildus in stillorgan when he was a teenager. And it was only a short time later when she was talking to someone about what had happened with the removal of the stone and the upset it had caused so many people. The person she was speaking to was attached to the school and after a short discussion it was suggested that perhaps it could be installed in the grounds of the school itself. But this would have to be put before the committee for approval before any further action could be achieved. We were all extremely excited with the possibility of this coming to pass. But although we waited in excited anticipation, we were also veering on the side of being cautiously optimistic to avoid any potential disappointment.

This was the originally setting of the memorial stone beside where he taught music. A small gathering of family and friends attended and a blessing of prayers by the local priest.

The passage of time went by. Weeks turned into months and we had to put this project to the back of our minds and move on with our lives. However one day Kitty received a wonderful phone call to inform her that her request to have the stone mounted in the grounds of the school had been approved and very shortly it was going to be placed in its new home. So beforehand when it was in its original setting only a few passers by could see this. And even then that was only if they were on foot and at very close proximity. As it is a very quiet residential area. But now in its new environment hundreds and over the next couple of years, thousands of people especially the young students will now be able to see this stone and appreciate the beauty and memory of the person it portrays. So you see we may have plans for ourselves but then God has bigger and better plans for our future which we may not be aware of at the time. So the next time an unpleasant situation arises in your life it could be trying to tell you something. You may have to re access where you are. To evaluate and stand back just a little and not to judge too quickly. To know that it is all happening the way it is meant to be happening. And yes it is difficult when we find ourselves in the midst of anything negative or destructive to see any logic or reason. But we have to accept that there are times when we are unable to do that. God's plans are for our highest good. And this for me was a good lesson to learn back then. Sometimes things *fall apart* so that bigger and better things can *come together*. Amist all the upset and confusion there was a better plan being worked out for the good of everyone concerned. And it exceeded our greatest expectations. Interestingly enough it was placed under a small Mountain Ash tree in the school grounds. In its original setting we had also planted a small Mountain Ash tree just behind it. Another coincidence who is to say. Also to mention here as an aside, that when I was organising the headstone for my husband there were two plaques printed out by mistake . In the grand order of things the second plaque would be placed beside the small inscription below which reads:

If I were a bird I would live in your branches
If I were a cloud I would hide in your leaves
If I were a breeze I would whisper in your ears
"I love you".

In loving memory of Owen.

I must say that I have met quite a few people during the process of writing this book who have told me how they have seen their deceased family members and friends. One lady recently told me how she had lost her only child a daughter eight years ago. She was only thirty and had type one diabetes. Unfortunately she had other complications and had gone into full renal failure and died suddenly. She and her daughter had been very close and enjoyed a happy family life. But following the tragic loss of her child this had led to the break up of the marriage and the family structure was gone. But there was this one time in the morning when the mother had woken up and she saw her daughter at the foot of her bed. I asked her was she in the stage between sleeping and being awake usually referred to as the 'twilight zone'. She was quite adamant that she was fully awake and she was stunned to witness the body of her daughter facing away from her towards a wall at the end of her bed. She sat up and could not believe her eyes. This lasted she said for a few minutes and then the image of her daughter disappeared. She went on to tell me that some people said the fact that her daughter was facing away from her was to let her know that she was departing this life. And also to convey the fact that she was alright. She continuted to tell me that she has many dreams of her daughter since and feels her presence with her all the time. It gives her great consolation and some respite from the physical loss.

Dr. Jean Jacques Charbonier a french anesthesiologist has studied psychic phenomena, mediumship and healing. His latest book "Seven Good reasons to believe in the afterlife." (In french). He is a well known afterlife campaigner in France having spoken at many conferences. During an interview in Toulouse with 'Lilou's Juicy Living European Tour', he talks to Lilou about his own experiences. The following is a sample of what he says during this interview: He argues that an altered state of consciousness is possible when the brain stops functioning. It is possible to establish true telepathic communication with a comatose person but also transmit thoughts. The spirit has been physically sensed leaving the body by many carers at the time of death. And he also experienced this himself when he was called to the scene of a bad car crash. The driver was still alive but had died shortly afterwards and he could *see* his spirit leave his body. A person in a coma is like an entity free from an earthly body and connected by a cord. This cord is referred to as 'the silver cord.' He believes that a life is possible in another dimension when physical death occurs and after the silver cord is severed. It is time to change the materialism scientific point of view he says. Certain ways of thinking in the past must change. He speaks about many testimonials of patients who have communicated near death experiences. It is the intangible the immeasurable aspect of these NDE which are similiar all over the world. Eighteen to twenty per cent of those people will tell you of their experience when they were pronounced clinically dead. They came out of their body. They could see what was happening around them and were fully aware and felt more *alive* then when they were in their bodies.

When they leave their analytical brain they are not sure what is happening. They go through a tunnel and they are not able to say where they are in time and space. They have one hundred per cent intuitive consciousness. When they come back to their bodies they feel a sense that their consciousness has diminished. That it has become smaller then when they were out of their bodies. They also report feeling very nostalgic and would prefere not to have come back to this earthly plain. Interestingly he said that he noticed that there was more automatic healing with the people who experienced an altered state of consciousness. He says we are going towards objectives that are more human. To share in helping others.

Some physicists are now saying that there could be another universe that we are unable to see operating at a higher vibration. Michio Kaku's who is a brilliant physicist, his explanation of dark matter is not only being a substance from another dimension in very close proximity to ours, but also consisting of strings (actually membranes) of a higher vibration. This is very key and interesting in how mystics describe astral matter as being a higher vibration and of another dimension. Could it be a similar frequency or universe where our astral selves go to when we die ? And if you take the example when we dream we are also in an altered state of consciousness which can allow and facilitate a connection with those who have passed. During sleep we ourselves reach a higher vibration and they in turn can lower their vibration and it is the thin space between the two vibrations which can allow communication to take place. So if subatomic particles can be in two or more places at once, could parts of us be travelling back and forth between universes and could these particles be dark matter?

Memorial stone in the grounds of Benildus school in Stillorgan for all to see. Above is the lovely Mountain Ash tree.

People who have had a near death experience describe being wrapped up in a beautiful light. It had the same feeling of home, family, reassurance and love. It was a true feeling of belonging which they have not found since. With this light came the feeling of incredible love and peacefulness. It felt like every cell of their body was being bathed in love on a molecular level. Sixty one per cent of people feel a strong emotional tone. They also experience a feeling of plural unity and understanding everything with extreme clarity all of a sudden. Like an internal and external ephiphany. Everything now makes sense. They have three hundred and sixty degree vision. As if they have eyes in the back of their head. Naturally because they are not in the confines of their physical shell anymore. Everything is heightened in relation to senses in human terms. But it is so much more than this and they find it hard to explain when they return. But the enormity and magnitude of it all they will never forget. They feel a sense of being claustrophobic when they enter their bodies again. A kind of imprisonment. That feeling of pure freedom and knowing can not be attained in the physical body. They try to discuss what their reality was when they had this NDE. One person described that they could see mathematical calulations in multi-dimension, describing how everything works in the universe. Magnetism, density, light, colour, and energy. It was amazing.

The following is a general overview dealing with people who have had these experiences. Forty eight per cent report a being composed of love. It created love, it emitted love, and it directed love. It was love. Twenty Six per cent report a landscape with flowers on the other side. These flowers glowed with indescribable colours. Also beautiful scents. Some report seeing a city with towers all in gold and white with wonderful bright colours. Twenty one per cent have a life review. From the time of their birth they see both good and bad experiences until the present. They also are the only one to judge their own actions. For example if they did something unpleasant to a person while they were living, they will actually experience the pain which the other person felt who they were interacting with. They have felt every detail of this. They could also see everything they had done throughout their whole life but much faster. This showed the good and the not so good. All they were proud of and those things which they were not so proud of in great detail again. Nineteen per cent of the people who had near death experiences were shown a vision of their future. They were shown people who they had not met yet and will later on meet. Plus different places where they will live.

The above information was taken from the International Association for Near Death Studies (IANDS). A sample of 787 (NDE) accounts date from 1960s to 2001. The sample was collected over the Internet, by mail and by verbal accounts around the world. The sheer number of cases, make this a valuable resource for researchers and investigators. The NDE contain many common elements. Two thirds report out of body experience, and almost as many see a light. More than half report strong emotional tone and receiving knowledge. Almost half report seeing unearthly beings.

PART II

WE ARE ALL ON A JOURNEY ONE OF DISCOVERY AND TRUTH

Chapter 8

WHEN SCIENCE AND SPIRITUALITY COLLIDE

Life Expands With Courage.

I like to say that what 'does not break us down – builds us up'. I was always told that no matter how bleak or dark one's situation may be you should focus on the fact that 'This too will Pass.....' You WILL turn a corner and the sun WILL shine again. Also 'If you find yourself in hell – keep moving.' There is a lesson to everything that happens to us in life. Perhaps despite a desperate situation where we know someone close is going to die, we can say that we were blessed to have had them in our life. That we have our own health. That is those of us who are blessed to be healthy. We can then get into the mindset of gratefulness and abundance in time. I have spoken to people who have lost someone close either suddenly or through a long debilitating illness. They are both tortuous events. Which one is the worst a sudden death or a long drawn out illness, knowing that the person is going to die. I think there are pros and cons to both situations. From the perspective of people *knowing* that their loved one is going to pass at the very least they are able to say goodbye and get their affairs in order. On the other hand people would say that they do not like to see their loved one suffer a long bout of illness. Both are true. With a sudden death which I encountered, my husband died in less than three minutes. No warning what so ever. He seemed in very good health. I did not get the chance nor did his children or his extended family to say their farewells and tell him how much we loved and appreciated him. On the flip side of this coin he did *not* suffer. He just passed peacefully. The only difference is with a sudden death I think it may be worse on the people who are left behind to pick up the pieces. The carnage of the sudden shock of it all. This really brought home to me how precious life is and how we should grasp it like gold dust.

Make our lives count for something. Find out what it is that makes you excited and motivated. For me now I feel it is through the medium of writing that I can convey my emotions and say what helped me move along the road to recovery. Out of that pit of bleak isolation to one of illumination and eventually enlightenment. Don't get me wrong I still get my bad days and very bleak days now and then like everyone else. But they are less frequent. They have less power and leverage over me. Very luckily for me I was and still am touched by Spiritual Experiences. I know not everyone is going to be that lucky and this is why I want to share what happened to me. If by my sharing my story will help to tell others out there who are in grief that there is light at the end of the tunnel. Life does continue on. 'Life After Life.'

It is at this time beyond our human understanding to be able to explain some of these events. One can get into Quantum Physics and Energy and so forth, but that means nothing if you have not experienced the other side for yourself. But it is never too late. To be always open to new experiences and communications. To watch out for the Signs they will let us know that we are never alone. I remember being in a hotel room last summer July 2010 with my daughter beside me in New York. The previous day I had been out with a friend and I was trying to remember the name of a particular actor. But being jet lagged and tired I was completely unable to recall the name. We were both approaching the subway and at the exact time of trying to think of the name I could see the steps of the subway directly in front of me. This in itself was normal and uneventful. However, later that night I was awoken by my husband's voice and this bright light around my head. He said and I quote "You made me smile when you were trying to think of the name of that actor on your way to the subway....." In my *dream* I could not believe that I was hearing my husband's voice. It was *real*, loud and crystal clear. I asked him "Do you love me?" and his reply was "Phyllis of course I love you - I will *always* love you." And the bright light which surrounded me went out and everything had gone dark around me again. I remember jumping out of bed and looking at the alarm clock on the locker between my daughter's bed and my own, it was 5.00am in the morning. I was wide awake. WHAT had just happened? I found this very emotional. I was totally moved. I began to cry. I could not help it. I did not want my daughter to hear me so I went into the adjoining bathroom and splashed cold water on my face. However she did hear me and asked me what had just happened. I could hardly explain it to myself never mind trying to explain it to anyone else. It was to me so *bizarre*. I began to tell her what had just happened. How her father's voice clear as a bell had woken me up from a deep sleep and how he began to relate an event from the previous day. He was obviously *with* me as I was making my approach to the subway, and when I *was* trying to think of the name of a particular actor. So this really got me thinking. I had never witnessed anything like this before. Another incredible lesson in communication. They are always with us. They obviously see what we do. That was proved to me. And they can read our minds. Any dream I ever had from loved ones were all of a telepathic nature. I never *saw* their mouths move as such but I did *hear* them speak. We do not have to understand something to have respect for it. And I had the utmost respect with the unknown nature of Spiritual Communication.

There was one other very curious encounter which touched my life recently. It was on July the 3rd, 2011 just the summer last year. I was having a despondent moment and had asked Owen for a sign out loud that day. "Could you make something move, or make a sound, just to let me know that you are with me ?" Nothing eventful happened for the duration of that day. And I forgot about my request. BUT, that night I had a dream. I found myself in this dream sitting on the edge of my bed as I had done so in previous dreams with my husband. He was sitting down on the bedroom floor talking to me. We both heard our daughter's door handle rattle and foot steps running down the stairs. I looked at Owen smilingly saying " I told you this house is haunted, you heard those footsteps too?" "Yes, I did" he said. Then continuing on in this dream he turned and pointed to where I have a small vent in my room and he said "Do you hear that crash?" And at the exact moment he said this to me in the dream I was awokened by a little noise or thud as if something had fallen against this vent. The noise had actually woken me up. Something had indeed fallen from the bed and knocked against it. It was one of my slippers which had fallen and knocked against it. Here was another *SIGN*. He *did* make something move, I *did* hear a noise and yes he was bringing it to my attention in this *dream*. He was with me. Another validation! Proof beyond measure. This did happen to me. I know what I experienced. I felt so privileged again to have been witness to something I could not fully explain but something I would gladly accept. Proof positive that there are answers occurring around us if we reach out and just ask. "Seek and you shall Find." My search was taking me on an exciting adventure. One I am still on and hopefully will be on for a long time to come. So now you may understand why I felt the compulsion to put pen to paper and write of my fascinating encounters. I had to share them. Is this not evidence that the essence of who we are as human beings continues on in another realm ? Is it not at the very least thought provoking on every level ? It cannot be dismissed out of hand through lack of any *physical* explanation. Intellect has somehow to be circumvented. We do not have the answers. And maybe we are not meant to. Who knows in time there may be further knowledge at our disposal to help determine exactly where we go after our bodies cease to function. Matter can never be destroyed only changed. Our minds and brains are separate. This has been shown in NDEs. When brain function ceases the person continues on in a different state only to come back and share their amazing encounters about loved ones who have crossed over before them. They are invariably told it is not their time. Most of them find it so incredibly beautiful that they want to stay there and not return to this earthly plain. But their life purpose on earth is not over. They still need to do what they were put here to do. Some accomplish this sooner rather than later. Others will need to live longer in order to fulfill their goal. There is an old Chinese proverb which says "The person who says it cannot be done should not interrupt the person doing it." By the same principle just because one has not experienced something Spiritual, they should not dismiss out of hand those of us who have been touched by anything Spiritual or by specific aspects of it.

Again we do not have to understand something in order to accept it. My mind is expanding to this concept. It fuelled my curiosity even more. I wanted to learn more and hear from people who had also had similar incidents happen in their lives. It felt so exciting.

Scientists are now delving into the world of consciousness and trying to determine what exactly is consciousness. One such scientist is Dr. Thomas Campbell – physicist. Dr. Campbell studied consciousness for over thirty five years. In laboratory settings he said consciousness is personal. You cannot get the fundamental nature of consciousness intellectually. He goes on to say that without sceptism one is not able to convert belief into knowledge. It is only experience which can do that. It is truly something you have to experience. I experienced several lucid dreams concerning my husband. Dr. Campbell says that Parallel processing goes on in lucid dreams. I can certainly relate to this. You know the times where you know you are dreaming and are also aware of your physical body. But 'you' your mind the intangible part of you goes into a different level a new dimension and your brain is observing this physically. Dr. Thomas Campbell has written a book called 'My Big T.o.e.' Toe standing for the 'Theory of Everything.' Einstein started the first theory. It was called the 'Unified Field Theory.' One set of equations which combined General Relativity and Quantum Mechanics. These are the two big areas of science which defines what reality is like. Our physical reality deals with Our Universe. The Normal, the Physical, and everything in it which is you and me. Dr. Campbell illustrates this on his website. He says that there is a Sub System – Physical Reality. Our Universe. In this Sub System he says you have Normal, Physical, Objective, and Matter. Then he illustrates to us on a diagram another system which is 'The Larger System'. This deals with the Paranormal, the Non physical, The Subjective Mind, Theology and so on. He says that consciousness exists and constitutes the larger reality which is taking the leap from one system to the next. He continues by saying that we evolve. That technology evolves. He mentions that we see consciousness as the System, and the Universe as the Sub-System. He says how do we define Non physical reality ? Non physical reality is a virtual reality. Albert Einstein said that "Reality is merely an illusion, albeit a very persistent one." Dr. Campbell says that Consciousness is not an objective system, is is a subjective system – it is inside each one of us. It is subjective so it is our own. It is not an objective thing. He continues on to say that reality concepts can be very slow to change. They require major paradigm shifts. This can be a lengthly process. To describe the non physical logically is hard. There has to be another huge level of reality which we do not fully know about.

Consciousness is the *media* of reality. Information is the *content* of reality. Information is non physical and so is memory. You need consciousness to get information. As regards to statistics and with so many people who have gone through paranormal experiences then the statistics become more concrete. I hope that with more scientists like Dr. Thomas Campbell studying this area, more credence will be given to people who have experienced and who will in the future experience the unknown. That a better understanding and a stronger validity will be shown to them. Also to be more respectful and tolerant and a little less judgemental. Many people keep these experiences to themselves for fear of appearing off centre or not particularly grounded when the opposite is the truth. With more and more people coming out and feeling more comfortable about the paranormal this will help to strengthen and reinforce the fact that it does exists. Some people just refuse to be convinced no matter how much evidence is put before them. But this close minded approach can be counter productive to those of us who are trying to make our stories heard. Therefore unfortunately as a result some keep it to themselves and question their own grounds on logic and what is real or not. Information is Power. The more information we have to hand will hopefully in time enlighten the world to what is going on beyond the five senses. And it does seem that globally there is a heightened awareness. More people are having fascinating encounters. This of course is spread more productively with the internet and mobile phones and the media as a whole.

There are now so many books written on the subject which will also continue to inform and teach people to be more open and receptive. This will help to shift the world's paradigm on the paranormal. Is there a reason why it seems that more and more people are having these interesting experiences at this moment in time? Is there a higher force out there which is trying to make its presence known perhaps? Are we getting a little closer to the biggest question of all time 'What happens when we die? Where do we go to? Do parallel universes exist? I would like to think that we are getting a little closer to some of these questions. But perhaps we are not meant to know the answers just yet. Perhaps we will get the tools and the knowledge to be more equipped to say what happens. There may be a right *time* for our questions to be answered. Hopefully we are approaching that time sooner than we think. I would like to think so. We need to be more receptive. As the saying goes 'When the student is ready, the teacher will appear.' We are the students. We need to listen. The lesson will be learned...

There was another very unusual and interesting experience which I had quite recently with my other child. My little boy Hugh has Down Syndrome and he is the delight of my life. He lives 'in the moment' and God knows there are so many books written on how to 'live in the moment.' But he does this *naturally* without thinking. He takes everything he encounters with joy and relish and has taught me positive lessons along the way. A good friend once said to me that 'they are our the greatest teachers' and I can certainly qualify this. He has been one of mine that is for sure. Always happy always keen to please and extremely empathetic. He *knows* when I am having a sad day or just feeling a little blue. He will do his utmost to make me smile or laugh. However, all this aside I mention his condition because he is also incapable of deception. More so because what I am about to tell you happened two years ago when he was only seven. Just to back up for a moment. He was three years old when his father passed on. They were inseparable. I used to call them 'Little and Large' like the comedy duo. My husband was six foot five and Hugh was tiny beside him and they adored one another. Owen used to say that he 'Is a different kind of Perfect.' We never saw his condition, we just saw *him* and his soul. No matter where my husband went he brought him everywhere and had him up on his shoulders carrying him proudly around which would delight the little fellow. So after my husband died my son was completely disorientated and confused. Where had his daddy gone. I had pictures of Owen around the house and he knew what he looked liked. But he was also feeling the sadness in the house following the death and also witnessed the absence of his father without knowing why. Why did he not see him in the house? Where was his best buddy? Well I always continued to talk to him about his father and we would look at photographs of him together. I certainly did not want to erase the memory of him just because he was out of sight. He was certainly not out of mind. Life continued on for the next three years as best as it could under the circumstances. It was a very difficult road but wonderful people had begun to enter my life and make my journey softer and give us hope again for the future. But as I mentioned earlier about two years ago my little son had crept into the bed beside me early one morning and the light began to fill the room. I had dozed off for a little while when my son began to grab my shoulder and say "Mama Dadda". I just thought he was thinking of his father and was wondering what could I say to comfort him. I just acknowledged what he was saying without paying much heed to it. But he was persistent. He kept on saying this. And then he put his two little hands gently on either side of my head as he leaned in over me and turned my head towards the wall which was opposite my bedroom window. He said again "Mama – Dadda!" And this time he was pointing to the empty wall getting very excited trying to convey to me his *mama* that he could *see* his daddy. I was so delighted for him. He started to wave and he was so delighted for those few precious moments. All I saw was an empty wall nothing else. And in case you are wondering if I had a picture of his father which he was pointing to on that wall, the answer is no. I had no pictures no representation whatsoever to remind him of his father. Just a blank wall with an old picture called 'The Shell Seekers ' which my father had given me several years beforehand.

Again I was witness to the unseen. I do believe that my husband was with us both early that morning in my bedroom. My little boy was certainly witness to that. I wished I could have seen him too but it was not meant for my earthly eyes. My little boy was the one who was meant to see him. And I was so happy for him. I greeted my husband like a blind person would greet someone familiar and much loved. But also like a blind person I was unable to see him like my son. I *felt* him and I *knew* that what had just happened was indeed a privilege denied to many. It gave me the impetus and motivation to move forward with the knowledge that my husband was indeed still parenting but from a different dimension. As I continue to grow spiritually, all that has touched me gives me strength and resilience to be more open to the unknown. It is just so fascinating. As I say I was not privy to what both of my children saw. My daughter was only fifteen months old and my little son only seven. And with his condition he was and still is incapable of telling lies or dressing up the truth. I know children can be histrionic a lot of the time. Having an imagination is second nature to being a child. But a baby and a young child with Down Sysdrome are not able to make up these types of experiences. You can be the judge of that. But I know what I know. It does at the very least make you wonder that there has to be more than what we see around us. Again there are so many forces which we CAN explain occurring within our physicality but are not able to see. Like electricity waves and electromagnetic waves and so on. Just because we cannot see them should we also dismiss them completely. Well we cannot. Because we KNOW they exist. The Paranormal by the same principle exists but with this we do not as such have a specifice measuring tool to come up with conclusive answers. There is a lot of speculation and theories out there to try and explain them away. But the truth of the matter is as of yet we do not have a definitive explanation to come up with the answers to some of the most baffling of events.

Owen loved his baby son whose unique difference and inner beauty was something he truly celebrated and respected. They went everywhere together and enriched each other's lives.

With love, acceptance, and nurturing, our little son is now a happy and productive child whose abilities are continually encouraged and developed. We are all special as human beings. Each one of us wants acceptance. To be validated and celebrated as individuals. To have our individualism shine should be our natural birth right.

Chapter 9

MAKING THE UNSEEN MORE VISIBLE

Faith is the substance of things hoped for
the Evidence of things not seen ....

The unexplained and the mysterious should continue to fuel our curiosity and our hunger for more information and knowledge. The more signs we receive the greater our impetus to seek awareness. In the meantime we just have to work on statistics world wide. The more people like myself who want to share their experiences and to relate that they *have* been visited by their loved ones. This will hopefully increase the belief and credence to what has happened to gain conviction. And should not be dismissed. You cannot argue with statistics. If they are huge in numbers they cannot be dismissed. There is something happening. A global awakening. Sometimes when I am watching a live coverage of something on television, be it a football match, a news report, or an Award Ceremony, even though you are not there *physically*, you are there in a different way. After all it is happening in Real time. You are observing it in Real time. You can see what is going on exactly as it is happening, but the people you are observing cannot see you observing them. Have you ever thought about that ? Just another 'food for thought'. I know in that instance the television is the medium which allows us to see things happening in real time. Without it we would not be able to capture events as they are happening. Also with the advent of mobile phones, this also enables us to see what is going on exactly as it happens. We are *there* with these people but just not physically. I think this is the closest concept to be observed by the Spirit World. They have the means to see us all the time. Like the live coverage analogy. We just cannot see them observing us. This may be one way of looking at this concept. I have also taken several photographs and seen Orbs. Also in other people's photos. They are said to be Spiritual beings. Interestingly Orbs do not show up on Professional cameras because professional cameras have hot mirrors to keep out low wave Infra Red Light.

Orbs fluorese from Photons expelled by the Camera's flash. They expand and then contract releasing low wave infra red waves which are then captured on regular digital cameras which do not have hot mirrors. When you see an Orb with hexagonal sides, it is because the leafed lens was closing at the exact time the Orbs were releasing its infra red waves, so the camera caught it with straight sides. I have a wonderful photograph taken of my little boy's first day at school. It was an emotional day for me like all parents with their children's first day of school. There are all kinds of emotions at play. One such emotion for me was not having his daddy there to share in this big occasion. I remember getting him all ready with his little shirt and jumper and taking a picture of him in my living room. He was sitting down with his back to the television. When I looked at the image after it was taken and printed there was a huge beautiful Orb just to the left of his head. I had taken another picture a few seconds later and the orb had vanished. When it was developed it was still there. I truly believe that his father was with his little son on his big day and this was his way of making his presence known. Since then I have seen many many Orbs but that one was the best of all. I also experienced a lot of flickering lights shortly after loosing Owen. I am told that when in Spirit, they are able to manipulate electricity and make lights behave in this manner. But the Orbs I find very interesting. And there are so many different types. There are big and small ones. Coloured ones. I took one photograph of my daughter and decided to take another one a few seconds later. In the first picture there was an Orb just to her left and again in the second picture taken only moments later it had moved to a different position. So they act independently from the observer. They are not dust clouds as the sceptics would like to say.

Dust usually does not look like orbs. Anyway, think of many internal photographs taken in one's kitchen or living room there is not the type or amount of 'dust' which could be explained away. Compared to a picture taken out of doors where there would be considerable more amounts and a different type of dust to perhaps on other occasions be passed away as this. A wooded or a ghost town from the old western scenario for example. A lot of dust are fibres. Orbs are not representations of dust particles as some may believe. Orbs are actually 'circles of confusion' (CoCs). CoCs are out of focus points of light caused by a reflection 'highlights' on dust particles. Highlights are everywhere. You can see clusters of highlights on almost any object when you have the light on is white. Because dust particles are so small they usually only have 'one highlight' that is reflected. It is this highlight, a pinpoint of light, that becomes out of focus and appears as an orb. This would help to explain why the colour and shape of an orb is not the colour and shape of dust. To explain what are CoCs a little further. In photography, a CoC is the smallest dot that a human eye can perceive in a photograph. When an object highlight is out of focus, this dot expands to become a recognisable circle. In the case of an out of focus dust particle caught in a flash, this circle is seen as an orb. The CoC size is usually around 0.05mm and can vary from camera to camera. Because dust particles are so small they usually only have one 'highlight' and thus produce just one CoC – or Orb. Larger objects have more than one highlight and thus can appear to be made up of a number of orbs. The distinction of an orb being "out of focus dust" and "a circle of confusion resulting from a highlight on a dust particle" might seem like a picky distinction in the greater scheme of things but it is not.

The fact that orbs are CoCs affects the colour and shape of orbs. Some people think coloured orbs are 'special' because they are not dust coloured and that oddly shaped orbs are 'special' because they are not the shape of dust. In reality no orbs are the shape or colour of dust. Orbs are the colour of the light reflected and the shape of the aperture of the camers. Orbs on stills cameras and camcorders were not identified and called 'orbs' until the mid -1990s. What we know as orbs did exist before this time but were so rare that they did not cause much if any notice in paranormal groups. Photographic evidence of orbs has been traced back to the early twentieth centure but none were published or linked with the paranormal until 1980 in Rickard and Kelly's *Photographs of the unknown*. This book defined the phenomena as unusual but natural. No other examples of pre mid 1990s orbs being linked with the paranormal have come to prominence yet. The effective discovery of orbs took place when suddenly, paranormal researchers were startled by orbs appearing on dozens of photographs of 'haunted houses'. This coincided with the mass production and distribution of digital stills cameras. Orbs quickly came to the attention by paranormal researchers in the years that followed. In 2002 there was a huge increase of paranormal investigation groups following the airing of the first season of UK cable TV show *Most Haunted*. Most Haunted made the assertion that orbs are the manifestation of spirits. Using an automatic compact camera your camera automatically makes adjustments for your decisions. The following different behaviours effect your Depth of Field DOF and therefore effect the size of the 'Orb Zone' and thus the number of orbs you photograph. If you are in an open, empty place your 'subject' will be far away e.g. (A wall or a tree) thus you have a greater DOF. Because of this greater DOF you increase the Orb Zone size and thus capture more orbs.

Taking photographs in the dark. If a location is really very dark the aperture will be larger, in order to draw more light, and the DOF will be shallower. The human eye works by the same principle. Therefore taking photographs in the pitch darkness will yield fewer orbs. Taking photographs in good lighting will produce fewer orbs, too, because the automatic flash will not activate. This information was taken from the Orb Zone: Orbs Explained. Virginia Hummel who has studied Orbs and taken over 10,000 photographs of Orbs has written a wonderful book called "Miracle Messenger: Signs from Above, Love from Beyond. This tells of a family's remarkable account about life after death. Virginia explains about why you do not see Orbs in Professional Photographs due to the professional cameras having hot mirrors to keep out low wave Infra Red Light. Virginia explains this very well. She has a web site called info-miracle messenger.com There does appear to be some sort of consciousness going on with Orbs. In so far as if you take a photograph and there is an orb present, and a second or two later you take the exact same photograph the orb has moved a little to the right or left, or has risen or fallen lower in the picture within a tiny time frame. Or perhaps it is absent. So taking this into consideration would certainly suggest that it has some kind of intelligence. We just do not fully understand exactly what they are. And again we can only speculate around their mysterious presence. But they can also be so beautiful. With different colours. Some people have even noticed *faces* inside some orbs. Even more fascinating. They will continue to fuel our curiosity until such a time arrives that we will be fully able to say definitively exactly what they are and how they come about. We may just have to be patient in the process. The PSI – Paranormal Site Investigators, and the ASSAP – Association for the Scientific Study of Anomalous Phenomena give more information on the study of Orbs for those of you who would like to investigate further.

Orbs are only one type of phenomenon which ignites our curiosity about the unknown and all things spiritual. However there are so many other avenues to explore when trying to deal in the area of the afterlife. Mediumship being another interesting and compelling study by observing without judgement. A recurring argument in psychic research is that the information produced by the medium can come from their own unconscious mind. Or from the mind of the person they are reading. But with genuine mediums neither telepathy nor their unconscious mind has anything to do with information transmitted from the afterlife. For those of you who seek further evidence of the afterlife the following is taken from The Book 4th Edition Chapter 16 - The Cross Correspondences. Just illustrating a small extract which deals with the work of Frederic Myers – Proof of Life After Death.: -

Frederick Myers was a founder of the Society for Psychical Research. Within a few weeks of Myer's death in 1901, he began to communicate through different direct writing mediums in England, the United States and India, sending information about what happens when we die. His scripts made no sense on their own but the mediums were told to forward them to a central location where they fitted together like a jigsaw. They were signed, "Myers."

The 'Myers Cross-Correspondences's have now become classic evidence for survival and are most influential and persuasive in helping many people come to terms with life after death. Frederick W.H. Myers was a Cambridge Classics scholar and writer late last century. He was also one of the pioneers who founded the Society for Psychical Research and was involved in investigation of the afterlife. When he was alive he was particularly interested to find a way of proving that information transmitted through mediums could not have come from their own unconscious minds.

The method he thought up was cross-correspondences -a series of messages to different mediums in different parts of the world that on their own would mean nothing but which when put together would make sense. He and his fellow leaders of the Society for Psychical Research felt that if such a thing could be accomplished it would have very high 'probative value' and be a high level of proof of continued existence. After Myer's passing in 1901 more than a dozen different mediums in different countries began receiving a series of incomplete scripts through automatic writing signed by Frederick Myers. Later there were scripts signed by his fellow leaders of the Society for Psychical Research, Professor Henry Sidgwick and Edmund Gurney, as they too had died.

The scripts were all about obscure classical subjects and did not make sense on their own. But when the mediums were told to contact a central address and the scripts were assembled, they fitted together like the pieces of a jigsaw as was mentioned earlier. In all, more than three thousand scripts were transmitted over thirty years. Some of them were more than forty typed pages long. Together they fill 24 volumes and 12,000 pages. The investigation went on so long that some of the investigators, such as Professor Verrall, died during the course of it and began communicating themselves. The mediums used by Myers and the others from the afterlife were not professors of the Classics.

They were not highly educated and all the messages were outside their learnt knowledge and experience. On one occasion one of the mediums, Mrs Coombe-Tennant, was conducting a discussion using 'automatic writing' between the spirit entity of Professor Sidgwick and his living colleague G.W. Balfour on the 'mind-body relationship' 'epiphenomenalism' and 'interactionism'. She complained bitterly that she had no idea what they were talking about and lost her temper that she was asked to transmit such difficult things.

The information transmitted in the Myers experiments was so accurate that it stunned the members of the Society for Psychical Research. At one stage those who were investigating the Myers Cross-Correspondences hired private detectives to put Mrs. Piper, one of the mediums involved, under surveillance. All the investigations proved her innocent of fraud or conspiracy or trickery.

The evidence is absolute. All the original documents are on file and there are at least eight complete sets of copies in existence for any investigator to study. One person who took time and effort to study the Cross Correspondences in depth was the former secular-humanist Colin Brookes-Smith. After researching them he states in the Journal of the Society for Psychical Research that survival should now be regarded as a sufficiently well established fact to be beyond denial by any reasonable person. Further he argued that this conclusion should not be kept in the obscurity of research records but should be presented to the public as :

A momentous scientific conclusion of prime importance to mankind. (Murphet 1990:64)

Myers had a strong interest in mediumship and tried to deal with and to understand the problems involved in interpreting its results. He was trying to prove that the mind of the medium could not be the creator of the message ie how could it be when the message was only a fragment which made no sense unless linked with other equally 'meaningless' fragments. And this is in reference to the

Cross-Correspondence. But when these messages joined up they made full sense. These pieces did more than refer to the same theme they did so in ways which were intricately intertwined. Those who studied and tried to interpret these 'jigsaw puzzles' called them cross-correspondences.

From 1901 to 1932 more than three thousand scripts were communicated. Receiving and interpreting such a large volume of material was often a huge task to those involved. But for Myers the whole enterprise was a one of struggle and anguish. He had survived physical death and now he wanted so much to communicate this fact in a way which would convince his colleagues who were still alive. But because he had no body he had to use the minds of others. He had to struggle to get through and convey his messages. And in the scripts he sent he refers time and time again to the suffering that this had cost him. After Myers passing he says that reality has two fundamental attributes – a physical and a psychic one. The physical is represented by a universe of matter located in a fixed space and time continuum. The psychic constitutes another complementary world which is not solid and fixed in matter, energy, space and time. Instead of being a creation it is creative. Instead of being an effect it is causative. Myers states that human beings reincarnate from the plane of illusion, but that once they have learned enough from periodic existences in the confines of this physical reality, they pass beyond these planes and need to be embodied no longer.

The Willett Scripts.
Another very convincing piece of evidence for the afterlife was provided by one of the mediums who had received some of the Myers communications. After her own death in 1956 at the age of eighty one Mrs. Coombe-Tennant, using her pen-name Mrs. Willett, transmitted a long and detailed book of personal reminiscences containing incredibly intimate detail about her own life through the medium Geraldine Cummins, who had never met her or her children. Published as Swan on a Black Sea the Willett scripts, as they are sometimes also known, are considered by many, including Colin Wilson, to be:

The most convincing proof of the reality of life after death ever set down on paper (Wilson 1987:183).

Colin Wilson, himself a former skeptic and now a writer with an international reputation did investigate. He writes:

Taken as a whole, the Cross Correspondences and the Willett scripts are among the most convincing evidence that at present exists for life after death.

The above information is just a sample taken from the web site Frederic Myers – Proof of Life and Death. For those of you who wish to read futher it is worth reading the full report which goes into greater detail and is thoroughly thought provoking.

These pictures were taken on my son's first day of school. A very special time for any parent in the lives of their children. It was poignant for me not having his father there on this special morning. I took the first photograph where he has the big smile. About a second later I took the second photograph. Here I zoomed out just a little and you can see the beautiful Orb beside his arm. The time difference in the two photographs would have been less than two seconds. The first is quite different. There is no Orb. I do believe his father was beside his little son on his special day after all.

Chapter 10
INTUITION AND SPIRITUAL AWARENESS

A gain the dreams and communications kept on rolling in from the 'Other Side.' One such dream which I did not pay particular attention to, was where my husband asked me the whereabouts of some important medical documents concerning myself and the children. They were very important in the event any of us needed medical attention. In my 'dream' I did tell him where they were and thought no more of it. But interestingly enough the very next day later I received a phone call from my doctor's surgery to inform me that they were two months out of date and to get these reviewed. I *never* knew this, but my husband did and was obviously trying to get my attention directed to this fact. Some would call this another synchronicity but the dream was too real to dismiss it as such. I hold true to the knowledge that I am being guided every step of the way. We all are. We need to pay attention to the signs which can be all around us. And for the first time in five years I am beginning at last to feel a degree of *internal* happiness. It is the best type to have. When it comes from within one's being. My soul I like to call it. I know I am on the right path. Where it continues to take me is still a mystery. But I am certainly enjoying the journey. I know I will reach the destination whatever that is. The early years following the passing of my husband had me in a constant state of anxiety and hopelessness. This being both an exhausting and depleting process. I felt like I had an invisible expanding void inside which nobody else could see. I thought back then I was falling into this and disappearing. Luckily for myself I have finally found the road back to recovery and renewal and the courage and strength to write this book. We all of us have this courage inside of us. We all need support. Family, friends, books and the media can be all helpful when we are in an emotional crisis. But we have to reach out and let others know that we are feeling vulnerable. We all wear masks. I did.

I wore different masks for different occasions. For family. With friends. With my children. But by the constant repetitive action of trying to be strong and appearing normal and in control, can be both emotionally draining and exhausting. Wearing the stoic *mask* over a long period of time will wear you down and postpone recovery and healing in the long run.

We may be fooling others for awhile, but we cannot delude ourselves and carry such a heavy burden for long. As Shakespeare said 'To thine own self be true.' Accept kindness wherever and whenever you can. People are wonderful and they want to help. Besides a few close friends most others assumed all was going well with me when the exact opposite was true. It was the wrong assumption. But I just kept plodding along and hoping that in time if I acted as if I was getting better then it should happen automatically. But life is not always that simple. So now if I am having a down or bad day I will let others know. And a good thought to remember is 'That this too will pass', and this too will pass ......' No matter how bad or harrowing a situation is, eventually that dreadful intense pain *will* subside. Again it varies from person to person. We are all different. And thank God for our individuality. And we all have something to bring to the table. Some tools which perhaps we have found helpful in the past we can therefore pass on to others who are going through a rough time. And in time when we come through that dark chapter in our lives it will give us an inner resilience and courage to move forward. To be a Survivor!

I must say I now feel truly blessed to know that I am not alone even when I may be physically alone. I know that my life here is still important and that I have work to do. The feeling and conviction through having my amazing connections via the medium of dreams has given me resolve and an inner strength to move forward again with an optimistic demeanor. I love the following quote: 'There have been no reports of Eye Strain from looking at the Brighter side of things.....' - optimism. I just love it. I also love the line I heard in a Rap song a few years ago which went something like *Faith is the Substance of Things hoped for, the Evidence of Things not seen.* How beautiful. Think about that sentence for a moment. And then say it a few times over again. It is so powerful and yet so simplistic. It really captures the essence of what faith is all about. The intangible. The unknown. The unseen. But for the lucky few they do get a glimpse. I definitely am not a medium. But I have been given the gifts from my amazing dreams to let me know that we *do* go on. Not everyone will be so lucky. Perhaps they may get a different sign. But at least by my sharing what has happened to me I can pass it on to others who need the consolation to know that they will see their loved ones again. They leave but they do not leave us behind. They physically leave and it is this which we all miss. For me it is the hugs. My husband was a big hugger and a gentle giant of a man. Extremely affectionate to everyone who came into his life. He always knew instinctively who needed a hug. They say we all need a certain amount of hugs per day to be happy and healthy! So give someone you love a big hug today. Please don't wait until tomorrow. Today is precious. Give your hugs away. They are very enriching.

Because I am quite petite in stature compared to my husband's large frame I always felt cushioned and protected with him by my side. And he always was by my side. There was such quiet reassurance when in his company. I loved linking his arm when we were walking out together. It felt like putting on your favourite wooly jumper and just being comsumed with its warmth. Be it a simple social walk out and about, or doing shopping or other necessary activities which had to be done. It did not matter. But it always felt the same. I suppose it was this one element which I found increasingly difficult after he died. Just the simple act of walking along a path by myself. Going *anywhere* by myself felt so strange and awkward. So I did not go out. Those of you I am sure can relate to these feelings too. I felt even lonlier when I was out. Everywhere I looked I seemed to be seeing couples. Young and Old. It was observing the old couples that I realised this would not be my future. This was robbed from me the day my husband died. And I felt angry and cheated. People used to ask me was I angry. And I would reply "Well Yes, but angry at the fact that I felt completely cheated and also my two young children were cheated of their father's presence. That was my mind set back then. I now know there is a reason and a specific timing for us to be born and to die. I started thinking that there must be something wrong in the grand scheme of things that it was me who was still left here. It was all very confusing back then. My mind was incapable of logic and I did not care. So I shrank deeper into myself. I loved the night time. That was my escape. To sleep. To retreat away from reality. I did not have to feel the piercing pain of grief which consumed my days. But sleep did not come easy. No not at all. Insomnia was my constant companion and my days grew even more weary through sleep deprevation. It was an endless cycle of apathy and emptiness. I became accustomed to the nature of merely existing but certainly not living. Everything appeared in black and white, the colour was slowly eroding from my perspective. I saw no joy in joyful things anymore.

That is what profound grief does. And nobody can explain this to you until it arrives at your door. Anyone of you reading this who has experienced the loss of someone very close can relate to what I am saying. People mean well. But if they have not been touched by this type of loss they are incapable to empatise fully. It is the most ravaging of feelings. I suppose looking back the two emotions which we can feel that we are truly alive is that of anger and sadness. So from that point of view I ticked those two boxes. But they are negative emotions which do not nourish or enhance our well being. We just have to go through them while on the road to recovery and in time try to become whole again. I am not the same person I was before my husband died. Part of who I was died five years ago as well. But I suppose I have grown into the person that I feel I was meant to be. I am a lot stronger. I do not take anything or anyone for granted. The small things in life if they go wrong do not bother me anymore. The important elements in life are the people you love plain and simple. The rest is all *things*. And most things can be replaced in time. But not a person. Never. And I have been awakened to the beauty and the fact that we are all doing the best we can in this life. It may not be other people's best, but it is our best. And never to stand in judgement of anyone for we don't know what it is like to walk in their shoes. What I say to others in my position or to anyone who has lost someone or something important. To appreciate what you have still intact in your life. It is not always the loss of a person that can diminish one's quality of life. It can be the loss of a job, a promotion, the loss of youth, the loss of a fantastic opportunity, or perhaps a high standing in society. They are all still losses and can have an equally devastating effect. But in time life will pull you along with it whether you like it or not. Change is part of life. It happens from the moment we are born. We change, people change, friendships change, and circumstances change. It is the law of nature too. The seasons change. We cannot do anything about this but try to embrace the positives which are within each type of change. And we in turn by effect, become ourselves changed. This can be both enlightening and a lesson in self discovery.

I think we as human beings by nature do not like change. Some more so than others. But we have no choice. So we have to adapt. We learn to take stock of our environment and then ourselves. And we may discover something new which other wise we would not know existed within each one of us. I have now realised that what I cannot change I just have to accept. Whether I like it or not. And this very fact can be very liberating. After all there is nothing we can do about a lot of the things which life can throw at us. So why worry about it. Now having said this, and being human of course it is easier said than done. But we can learn to circumvent negative situations by using techniques which are helpful to us as an individual. When we learn, we expand. And I am talking here about Comfort Zones. We all have them. But if we do something small each day that will take us out of our comfort zone the ripple effect of our existence will be bigger. Like throwing a stone into the water, the bigger the stone the bigger the ripple effect will have on the water. And so too it is with our behaviour and risk taking. Some will pay off, some may not. But at least we have tried and we expand our actions in trying for similar or bigger risk taking. At least you can say you have tried. But if you never take the risk you will be always wondering if that opportunity you so wanted to happen would have materialized or not. So give it a try. You could be very happy with the results!

As I was explaining earlier the comfort I used to feel being the other half of a couple. I did feel complete in myself as an individual. But there is also the added bonus of being with another who validates and understands who you are. And going out as a couple was always delightful. Just walking by myself felt strange and self conscious for a long time. I missed the companionship and the sharing of ideas and activities which touched my day. Back in May 2008, only two short years after Owen passed, I had yet another one of my *dreams*. I really prefere to call them *communications* from the other side. Anyway, to continue I had this dream where I found myself walking beside my husband down a deserted and dusky street near where I live. There was nobody else around just the two of us. My husband was wearing his long woolen dark coat which he wore alot when he was alive. I was linking his arm as I used to do and I looked up and said "This is what I miss." Then I put my hand into his coat pocket and said "This is also what I miss as I *felt* the warmth of his hand which he had in his own coat pocket. We continued to walk along the street in the dream. He never spoke but just looked down at me and gave me a big smile. There was alot of reassurance in his countenance. And that was it. Brief but again something I was still able to enjoy and experience as I had done many times when he was alive. It is the simple things about a person which you miss the most when they leave. The little things which makes us all unique and special. Which defines us as individuals. This is hard to leave behind when they are no longer around physically. But nobody can take away the memories. They will live on forever. It is dealing with the loss of the person's characteristics which makes the lonliness very hard to come to terms with.

Dreams are truly the main and most effective method of communication between this life and the hereafter. And it is these dreams which set themselves apart from the other types of dreams we would usually have. The clarity of detail is much greater. The person remembers having them with a stonger recall. Elements like temperature, facial expressions, being able to *interact* with the people are usually reported with these dreams. They are more tangible in their substance. They appear to be very real and easier to recall. It is not always easy to consciously incubate a dream. They can be disjointed and illogical. Sometimes with little or no apparent reason. These variety of dreams are a rich source of enlightenment for the dreamer. They are spiritually enhancing in their nature too. A source of inspiration. Such artists who credit dreams as a source of inspiration, include the poet-painter William Blake, painter Paul Klee, and screenwriters Judith Guest and Ingmar Bergman. George Frederic Handel claims to have heard the last movements of his famous oratorio *The Messiah* during a dream. Some dreams come from a spiritual realm and these dreams have spiritual characteristics. Dreams happen all the time but sometimes we have one that leaves us feeling like it was almost real. When we sleep our minds are quiet and totally receptive to spiritual messages. Besides meditating it is the one time each day when you can receive signs from God or whoever has passed over. You can receive your divine message. If you can keep a written diary it will be easier to track down a theme or something significant which applies to your life. Dreams which also produce a strong emotional tone and feeling are considered to be spiritual. Then when you put your own interpretation into the dream you will hopefully gather more information. When the dream produes a dramatic emotional feeling of love, sadness, fear or any strong emotion you should pay special attention to it. There will usually be a strong component or a message which will stand out the most in your dream. You should take some time to figure out the message. One such dream which had a very strong emotional tone for me was back in November 2004. In this dream I found myself in a waiting room of sorts. I was aware that the people around me were gravely ill. This was the strong vibe I was feeling from the men and women in this dream. In this *waiting room.* I was at the back seated behind many rows of very sick people. I could see and sense this from their appearances and everything *about* them. Then I heard my voice being called behind me. When I turned around I saw my father and seated beside him was was grandfather who had passed on when I was six years of age. I remember vividly within this dream getting a strong sense of dread and sorrow. My father in the dream was asking me why I was here. And keeping in mind during this time he was very ill in hospital after having cardiac surgery. He had also suffered two strokes and was not expected to live very long. To continue with my dream. I turned to my father and then began to stare at my paternal grandfather who was staring at me with a gentle smile. He never spoke to me. I remember within this dream being extremely surprised to see my grandfather looking so well and his features so well defined and looking serene and handsome. He never took his eyes from mine. And I said to him: "How lovely to see you it has been *so* long." He continued to smile without speaking and I got this strong sense that he was beside my father preparing to help him to cross over. I instinctively became strongly aware that my father was going to die very soon. Perhaps this dream was a preparation for me to be prepared for the enevitable prospect of loosing my own father shortly. And again it woke me up. The emotion was raw and sorrowful. Again the tears began to fall from my eyes. Owen woke up beside me and I told him about the dream and the fact that I saw my grandfather sitting beside my own father. Receiving the strong sense that he was coming to help his son cross over. It was such an intense feeling of impending sadness. I just could not shake it off. Three months later in February the 17th, 2005 my father did pass on in hospital. I now believe that this dream was to prepare me and to issue an early warning signal of this expected outcome with the loss of my father.

Sometimes spiritual dreams can occur more than once if they are trying to impart a message. And dreams which give you information or allow you to learn something occur during times of spiritual advancement or as messages. Some spiritual dreams awaken senses that are normally closed off to us in the dream world. You could experience *taste*, to *feel* or the sense of *smell*. *Feel* the wind in your hair which happened to me in a previous dream. Be able to smell a flower, feel the rain and touch your surroundings. All very real but still in the dreaming state. Also the sense that you are being drawn to a bright light. This light can appear overwhelming but it still draws you to it. I also experienced this type of dream when I was in New York in the summer of 2010. These dreams awaken our senses which we would normally not experience in the other regular type of dreams. Dreams in general can create seeds of great creativity and lead to a certain level of awareness and clarity over time. But the more I began having dreams where I connected with people who had passed over, the more spiritually aware I was becoming. A heightened sense of being open to signs around me. More receptive as a channel. And I wanted to learn more and to try to understand what was occuring. Also with dreams and with the prophetic many things are symbolic. There are many books written on the symbolism of dreams. One rule in biblical study is to let the word interpret itself. But with the nature of dreams being subjective to each one of us, we are naturally going to see the dream as it relates to our own life and with those we interact with. We will consciously or subconsciously put our own connotations from the content of our dreams. With patience and practice we may be able to see a pattern emerging which could be a guiding beacon in certain aspects of our lives. But at the very least, we should try and listen to what it is our dreams could be trying to tell us.

The following is a poem by Edgar Allan Poe on dreams.

Dreams.

Oh! that my young life were a lasting dream.
My spirit not awakening, till the beam
Of an Eternity should bring the morrow,
Yes! Tho' that long dream were of hopless sorrow,
'Twere better than the cold reality
Of waking life, to him whose heart must be,
And hath been still, upon the lovely earth.
A chaos of deep passion, from his birth.
But should it be that dream eternally
Continuing - as dreams have been to me
In my young boyhood – should it thus be given,
'Twere folly still to hope for higher Heaven.
For I have revell'd, when the sun was bright
I' the summer sky, in dreams of living light
And lovliness have left my very heart
In climes of my imaging, apart
From mine own home, with beings that have been
Of mine own thought - what more could I have seen?
'Twas once and only once- and the wild hour
From my remembrance shall not pass – some power
Or spell had bound me – 'twas the chilly wind
Came o'er me in the night, and left behind
It's image on my spirit – or the moon
Shone on my slumbers in her lofty noon
Too coldly – or the stars – howe'er it was
That dream was at that night- wind - let it pass,
I have been happy, tho' in a dream.
I have been happy – and I love the theme.
Dreams! in their vivid colouring of life,
As in that fleeting, shadowy, misty strife,
Of semblance with reality, which brings
To the delirious eye, more lovely things
Of Paradise and Love – and all our own!
Then young Hope in his sunniest hour hath known.

Edgar Allan Poe

Chapter 11
GAINING HOPE THROUGH THE POWER OF DREAMS

Crossing over is not extinguishing the light, it is putting out the lamp because dawn has come.
- R. Tagore.

The energy of the mind is the essence of life' - Aristotle. If you think about this sentence for a moment, its truth is resounding in its simplicity. If our mind is empty, devoid of direction or purpose and filled with negativity, we are truly unable to move our lives forward with any sense of conviction or goal. With the mind, we are what we think. Just like with our bodies, we are what we eat. Thoughts are extremely powerful. If we believe them to be true whether they are good or bad, we are giving them permission to affect our lives. And with this mindset our behaviours in turn will be effected. Only ourselves have the ability to change. Nobody else can do it for us. People can offer advice and give guidance, but we have to be open to accepting this advice in order to move on and heal. If we remain closed in emotionally it is harder to crawl out of that pit of depression. Our comfort zone becomes smaller and we are more apprehensive in taking any step forward. It takes as long as it takes. It is a very individual process. It cannot be hurried. But it has to happen. It is both an internal and external one. The most productive and empowering one is when it comes from within. For me this was what happened. I had an epiphany. I received great strength and courage from within. I was and still am spiritually touched and blessed. As the following saying shows : 'There is a Supreme Power and ruling force which pervades and rules the boundless universe. You are a part of this power.' - Prentice Mulford.

Sometimes we need to trust our inner voice our instinct. Some would call it the Higher Self. Whatever you want to call it it is there and can become more evident over time. To trust and let go. Other people like to say 'to trust and let God.' Patience is the key here. I never thought for one moment I would reach the level I am currently at. And when you are in that dark place you feel you are unable to move forward in any respect. This could also be called Intuition. Intuition is very interesting and worth talking a little more of here. Intuition is the ability to acquire knowledge without reference or the use of reason. The word 'intuition' comes from the Latin word 'intueri', which is often roughly translated as meaning 'to look inside' or 'to contemplate'. Intuition provides us with beliefs that we cannot necessarily justify. For this reason, it has been the subject of study in psychology, as well as a topic of interest in the supernatural. Intuition is commonly discussed in writings of spiritual thought. Intuition is regarded as a conscious commonality between earthly knowledge and the higher spiritual knowledge and appears as flashes of illumination. By definition, intuition cannot be judged by logical reasoning. Thomas Merton discussed variations of intuition in a series of essays. In describing aesthetic intuition he asserted that the artist has a subjective identification with an object that is both heightened and intensified and thereby "sees" the object's spiritual reality. In discussing Zen meditation he asserted that a direct intuition is derived through a "struggle against conceptual knowledge." An end result is "the existent knows existence, or 'isness,' while completely losing sight of itself as a 'knowing subject.' Empathic accuracy is a term in psychology that refers to how accurately one person can infer the thoughts and feelings of another person. It was first introduced in conjunction with a new research method by psychologists William Ickes and William Tooke in 1988. It is similar to the term *accurate empathy*, which psychologist Carl Rogers had previously introduced in 1957. Empathic accuracy is an important aspect of what William Ickes has called "everyday mind reading." INTUITION may be defined as understanding or knowing without conscious recourse to thought, observation or reason. Some see this unmediated process as somehow mystical while others describe intuition as being a response to unconscious cues or implicitly apprehended prior learning. - Dr. Jason Gallate & Ms Shannan Keen BA. Intuitive people are highly aware of other people's emotions. They have a deeper understanding of themselves, or their environment. How other people work. Highly Intuitive people are called Sensitives. They are generally more alert. They know how to figure out and understand what is next. If you think you are intuitive you can be ahead of everyone else. You have figured out things before other people have become aware of them. You are picking up on information.

Sensitives can become easily overwhelmed. They are drawn a lot towards helping other people. Also more drawn to the healing arts. Then intuitive abilities and deeper psychic senses become more apparant. The opening signs to being an intuitive is that there is an increase in coincidences. Things or events happening at the right time and the right place where you will find yourself. Or you may be picking up on some information which you were thinking about for some time and suddenly it happens in front of you. Also thinking you *see* things moving from your peripheral vision and then looking and not seeing anything. Another sign is dreams of events before they actually happen. You are opening up to different vibrations and energies before they become physically manifest in the everyday world. Strangers will start opening up to you and tell you important moments which have deep meaning to them. You can be minding your own business it does not matter. They will be attracted to confiding in you. Also some intuitives find themselves drawn to certain colours. Pink or lilac or white are the common colours. Are more sensitive to noise. Will prefer quiet and solitude. It just feels easier. It is not just a preference. I came across a new word while I was doing my research for this book. Perhaps you have or have not heard of it. It is called cryptesthesia. It literally means "hidden sensation." It refers to information gathered by the senses that enters conscious awareness by some other form. The waking awareness generates a narrative based on the sensory input it receives. Input deemed relevant is frequently ignored or stored for later within the mind. Sometimes the mind recognizes the need for that information.

There have been so many books and films produced using the theme of the Sixth sense. But we all have it. Call it what you will. I suppose we do not use it as much now compared to our ancestors back when the dinasours were roaming the earth. It was a matter of life or death back then not to be finely tuned into this sense. But nowadays we are not in daily situations of 'fight or flight' as much. You know the feeling you get when you are in an area or a neighbourhood where there may be social problems etc. You have the *feeling* perhaps not to go down a certain alley or street because it does not *feel* right. I think we have all had that feeling at some stage It is alerting us to the unseen dangers which are around us. But with modern technology and the advancements in science and so on we are not as exposed to these dangers now as much as we were a century or so ago. We are travelling in moderate safety. We do not have to do as much walking as our grand parents. People just hop in and out of cars so we are not as vulnerable as pedestrians if we find ourselves in an unsavoury or dangerous predicament. So sometimes we ignore our inner voice our innate warning system which tells us that something is not right. Move on or get out. We should become re acquainted with our sixth sense. It is still important. In more recent psychology, intuition can encompass the ability to know valid solutions to problems and decision making. For example, the recognition primed decision (RPD) model explains how people can make relatively fast decisions without having to compare options. Gary Klein found that under time pressure, high stakes, and changing parameters, experts used their base of experience to identify similar situations and intuitively choose feasible solutions. Thus, The RPD model is a blend of intuition and analysis. The intuition is the pattern matching process that quickly suggests feasible courses of action. The analysis is the mental simulation, a conscious and deliberate review of the courses of action. Neurobiologist Roger Wolcott Sperry said that though intuition is a right brain activity while factual and mathematical analysis is a left brain activity. People have different perspectives on Intuition. One such perspective comes from Abella Arthur. 'Intuition is a combination of historical (empirical) data, deep and heightened observation and an ability to cut through the thickness of surface reality. Intuition is like a slow motion machine that captures data instantaneously and hits you like a ton of bricks. Intuition is a knowing, a sensing that is beyond the conscious understanding '.

Carl Gustav Jung said that 'Intuition (is) perception via the unconscious.' Jung also said that a person in whom intuition was dominant, an "intuitive type", acted not on the basis of rational judgment but on sheer intensity of perception. An extraverted intuitive type, "the natural champion of all minorities with a future", orients to new and promising but unproven possibilities, often leaving to chase after a new possibility before old ventures have borne fruit, oblivious to his or her own welfare in the constant pursuit of change. An introverted intuitive type orients by images from the unconscious, ever exploring the psychic world of the archetypes, seeking to perceive the meaning of events, but often having no interest in playing a role in those events and not seeing any connection between the contents of the psychic world and him – or herself. Jung also thought that extraverted intuitive types were likely entrepreneurs, speculators, cultural revolutionaries, often undone by a desire to escape every situation before it becomes settled and constraining - even repeatedly leaving lovers for the sake of new romantic possibilities. His introverted intuitive types were likely to be mystics, prophets, or cranks, struggling with a tension between protecting their visions from influence by others and making their ideas comprehensible and reasonable persuasive to others - a necessity for those visions to bear real fruit. By following through on everyday hunches you are honing in on your listening skills. The more we do this the more fine tuned we will be to this side of us. Intuition is the ability to get a sense, vision or feeling about someone or somebody. It communicates with us through symbols feelings, and emotions. Its language can be hazy and unclear. We used it more when we were children. As adults, our rational and reasonable mind develops. We ignore it. Listening to your intuition is the essence of art and creativity. We can try to recapture this by meditation. By focussing on an object or the flame of a candle can help our mind to steady itself and other thoughts from creeping in to disturb our attention. Try to remember what comes into your mind and write it down if possible. It is not always guaranteed you will remember everything. 'The faintest ink is better than the strongest memory.'

Through meditation we can connect more efficiently with our loved ones who have passed over, and who in turn will be able to touch our existence on this plain more tangibly. This is another huge side of ourselves that we can explore and if we can expand our sense to what is *possible*, then being able to experience that is the HIGHEST form of discovery. Carl Jung said the following quotation : "I regard intuition as a basic psychological function that mediates perception in an unconscious way. Intuition enables us to divine the possibilities of a situation ....." Jung also said that intuition is one of four major functions of the human mind along with sensation, thinking, and feeling. By balancing all of these functions within ourselves, we have the ability to maximize our potential. Albert Einstein said: "I never came upon any of my discoveries through the process of rational thinking." Very interesting isn't it. Think about it for a moment. This could be said to being 'Inspired' from above. This is where the word *Inspiration* comes from. 'In- Spirit'. A combination of a deep innate feeling of *knowing* something to being true without having the facts beforehand. We all have this ability. Some more than others. But it can be cultivated and enhanced with practice. It can even save your life. Just knowing that a particular situation or person is not for your highest self or benefit. To go with your gut or intuition from within. You could say it is like our inner guidance mechanism. An instinctive knowing which neither requires, nor employs logical thought processes. It is an alternative source of knowledge, a level of awareness. Our inner voice. It can help in your professional life and in all areas of your life. By listening from within will effect what is on the outside of our being. Immanuel Kant emphasized the importance of intuition and the great impact it had on his personal and professional life. He defined it as a 'priori' knowledge, and as being an essential and indispensable tool for us all. Intuition is also a means of creative self expression, especially in the world of art, music and literature. Nor, is it restricted to the creative arts. In the area of science, business and entrepreneurship many have achieved remarkable success. These people have achieved their success by trusting their own intuition and their abilities to make important decisions by following their hunches, or gut feelings. Our subconscious mind uses our intuition to connect the two. It is how the conscious mind is communicated by the subconscious mind. Hence the amazing source of wisdom, creative power, and understanding which emanates from our subconscious mind. It does transcend the realms of reasoning and experience. It is a source all of its own and a very powerful one at that.

It is worth developing your intuition. There are many reasons for this. As I just mentioned it helps to connect you with your own subconscious and discover hidden truths about yourself and your own situations in your life. You can then hopefully prevent the accumulation of negative emotions and negative thinking. As a result you will be better able to make more effective and more positive decisions. It also improves your overall physical, mental, and emotional health. So those reasons by themselves are surely a good grounding to start this wonderful and enlightening exercise. All you need is a few minutes of quiet time alone. You will be more productive to yourself and to those around you who love and support you. It is important to let others know that this is something you need to do. If they understand the importance of this in your life, they may also be able to facilitate you being more productive in carrying this out. You may also find yourself becoming more creative and using your imagination more effectively and in different ways which you never did before. And the best point of all is that your stress levels will decrease. The main reason for this is that you will be able to identify and deal with your problems more effectively and efficiently. This all leads to a better quality of life. The more you practice like everything else in life, the better you will be at it. Start off slowly and gradually over time you will increase your intuition. It is a skill like any other. It also integrates the left and the right brain function. This gives you a more complete perspective on dealing with everyday issues and events. Improves your power of perception and judgment on people and incidences which arise in your life, big or small. *To develope your Intuition skill.* You must be in a quiet space. Turn off any distractions like radios, television, mobile phones and so on. Make sure that you are sitting comfortably and that the temperature is not too hot or too cold. Otherwise this in itself will disrupt any chance of progressing. Sit still and just *listen.* Try to experience the silence around you. Clear your mind by using any technique you find or have found to be a useful tool for this. Don't expect anything. If a thought comes into your head just let it. Be open to what happens. Maybe nothing will for the first few times. When you begin to listen to your intuition it connects you with a greater knowledge. It can communicate with you through symbols emotions or feelings. You may get solutions to problems you have been battling with for awhile. You may get flashes of insight and wonder *where did that come from?* Keep on doing this everyday for as long as you practically and comfortably can. And in time you will find that there is an inner voice you instinct, your higher self guiding you on the correct path and giving you the right answers. You just have to LISTEN.

In order to increase intuition and your intuitive abilities, you must pay attention to what is going on around you. We are all constantly bombarded with information on a daily basis. From the media and the people around us. Our conscious minds can reach saturation point at times. And the more information we are taking on consciously, the more your subconscious mind has to work with when it comes to making an important decision. Since your intuition uses the information gathered by the conscious mind, the more you have available, the better the solution. Understanding and knowledge which comes from experience helps to add quality of insight provided by your intuition. The Subconscious mind communicates information to the Conscious mind through your intuition. Other types of intuition reveal themselves in inspiration or thought flashes. Just be observant to this. And take heed. The more you pay attention the more of these *flashes of insight* you will experience. I'm sure we can all remember a situation where by we ignored our gut instinct and went against our better judgement just to have an unpleasant circumstance develop as a result. So to prevent these negative incidences from occurring less frequently, make sure to pay attention to the smallest of signs or inner feelings you receive. If you have an important question in your life which you need guidance or direction on, a good time to employ your subconscious is just before you fall asleep and while you are actually sleeping. Think of what it is you would like or a particular question you need to have answered and then explore different possibilities. This will trigger your imagination and put your subconscious to work at providing you with creative solutions while you sleep.

It is also a good idea to have a pen and paper ready to write down any great ideas or answers which may have presented themselves to you that night. Write them down. Even the content which may not have much clarity or may seem convoluted, but in time could be revealed. Again you could be dealing with symbols which could in the future reveal themselves and become more distinct. Another way of tapping into your Intuition is by keeping a Journal. When you write you tap into your thoughts, feelings and ideas which you may not be usually conscious of. This is a wonderful way to extract your inner messages, insights, or any hidden knowledge about a situation or problems which require you to solve. It is certainly worth the try. And you could be very pleasantly surprised at the positive results. Some of the following quotes on Intuition are very good and I would like to share them here. They also have great wisdom and simplicity combined. I think it is this combination which when employed can make them extremely effective.

The following quotations on Intuition are:

"The two operations of our understanding, intuition and deduction, on which alone we have said we must rely in the acquisition of knowledge." - *Rene Descartes.*

"Intuition is a spiritual faculty and does not explain, but simply points the way." - *Florence Scovel Shinn.*

"All perceiving is also thinking, all reasoning is also intuition, all observation is also invention." - *Rudolph Arnheim.*

"Trust your hunches. They're usually based on facts filed away just below the conscious level." - *Dr. Joyce Brothers.*

"When intuition and logic agree, you are always right." Anonymous.

When I first became aware of the Spiritual side of things I was confused and on unfamiliar ground. Going about everyday life like we all do that was enough in itself to keep me busy and focused. But with this new awareness which started over fourteen years ago when my daughter was only fifteen months old, I knew a whole new world existed beyond my five senses. We tend to use logic and rationale to explain away the unknown. But sometimes there are no apparent answers to which we can conclusively give a definitive answer to. I certainly could not. But again, my curiosity was fuelled to take heed to what was happening around me. To try and find out more if I could. When we try to solve something whatever it is, we are thinking critically. We depend on reason over the emotion. Like Modern art sometimes you do not always understand it, but merely react to it. The interpretation is unique to each one of us. And with the paranormal the same principle can be used. We have a predisposed idea on nearly everything in life. But with the area of the unknown we have to put aside personal biases and prejudices. Then we are able to consider all reasonable possibilities. Having an open mind is crucial to this. To being open to alternative interpretations without getting too bogged down on details. We can expand our knowledge with books and other people's experiences with similar occurring events. Enlightenment may or may not come quickly. And this is where Intuition can play a big part which I have just spoken about previously. Like the analogy of an open door, the more open it is the more that can come in. Or by the same token the wider you open a window, the more light and air can come through. And so too by the same principle applies with our own minds. If we can open up the mind, it will expand to facilitate knowledge and energy from new dimensions and horizons which were previously hidden from view.

The expression having a 'Closed Mind' is so true. We have to open ourselves up to the mysterious and the new. That is true liberation. Otherwise we end up by going around in circles. We have the power to choose our perspective and our thoughts. But sometimes what can come into our mind is outside of ourselves. Beyond ourselves. Not all situations in life have a solution. And when we deal with the area of the Paranormal that is the case at times. Just to accept the situation for what it is and move on. We can then see them as opportunities to challenge our thinking and the world's paradigm. And the world view on the supernatural is shifting already. Due to more people coming forward and telling their own personal story, as I have shared my own. There is more acceptance and a keener sense to know more. The *mystique* is starting to diminish.

Perhaps still in my lifetime there will be more advances in science to explain away some of the remaining mysteries which still continue to defy logic. I think we just change into a different State when our physical bodies die. Like water. At 211 degrees it is very very hot. At 212 degrees it boils and then becomes steam. It is not that the water is destroyed but merely changed into a different *state*. Matter cannot be destroyed only changed. Also at extreme degrees below zero, water becomes ice. Another state, changed but not eliminated. We are all energy. Our thoughts are energy. Our thoughts can effect our attentions and those around us. Body language experts will tell you that we mainly communicate in how we hold our bodies and how we position ourselves in relation to those we interact with on a daily basis. The voice is only a small portion of this. Death is not annihilation it is a change of State. The Ultimate change of state.

Chapter 12
WONDEROUS CONNECTIONS

"I ask not for a lighter burden, but for stronger shoulders."
- Jewish Proverb.

L ord Byron said that 'Adversity is the first path to truth.' I found this to be the case when I lost my husband. I encountered many losses in a short space of time. My three babies through miscarriage. The loss of my father. Then the loss of my husband. All uniquely harrowing in their own individual ways. One loss does not prepare you for the next, nor does it soften the blow of a new bereavement. We are not made that simple. We are complex and our grief can run deep. But with every death I experienced an emotional wound growing bigger and deeper with each loss. It was an internal void which nobody could physically see. A big gaping hole and I felt like I was falling down deep inside of this. But I remember hearing somewhere that it is only where there is emptiness and darkness that the healing and positivity can come through and fill up this vaccum. If there is no space no opening then nothing can enter. So over time and I mean several years this vast hole within my being was being filled in by a 'Spiritual Substance.' An awareness which was beginning to make me feel whole and alive again. I cannot fully explain it but I felt it. Slowly at first, and then it was more tangible. Yes my heart was broken but at least I was like the walking wounded. I was starting out again. Baby steps in the beginning. But I was moving forward. And bit by bit, piece by piece my resolve was starting to grow. And it is in this early stage that we have to be kind to ourselves and not expect too much too soon. Not to compare our situation with another's. We all react differently and with different strengths. Each will climb their own mountain in their own good time.

The dept of grief is relative to the relationship you had with the deceased. For example loosing a parent or a spouse would have deeper significance and a deeper sense of loss than loosing a distant cousin or an aunt who you have not seen in years. So bereavement can vary from a slight feeling of regret to downright incapacitation if the person was a very big influence and enriching force in your life. Also we each have our own coping skills and ways to circumvent the verocity of grief. Let nobody say it is easy. Or "You will be just fine – time is a great healer." You do not want to hear this when you are in the depths of despair and loss. A tornado has just swept emotionally through your life and picking up the pieces of a shattered existence can be a monumental task to say the least! Those lucky enough who have not experienced a deep loss are not able to relate to such devastation. And who can blame them. I was the same. I would sympathise and be there for those who had lost significant others in their lives, but not having had that same experience, I was unable to empathise, to *feel* the enormity of their loss. It is like everything else in life. Unless you walk in another person's shoes we should never cast judgement or criticise that person. Each of us has our own cross to bear and at times the burden can seem just a little too heavy. But I like to call myself a Survivor. I really feel like a solder who has encountered many emotional battles, but have emerged out the other end. Wounded yes, but a survivor none the less. If I can do it with many adversities one after the other, so can YOU. Getting a good support system around you is crucial. It does not have to be a group. But just ONE person who wants to listen and just 'be there' for you. When and where you need that person to be. Sometimes you may not feel like touching base with this friend or confidant but that is alright. Just the *knowing* that there is someone at the other end of a phone who understands where you are at psychologically and emotionally. It is a wonderful feeling. I was very blessed to have a few such people in my desperate state of need. The first to be with me and who could empathise was a wonderful lady who many years before was also left a young widow with a three year old little boy. She was the Chaplain at my little boy's school. And she came every single week to be with me and listen to my grief and feelings of utter hopelessness. She was an instrumental part in my healing and we have become and remained good friends to this day. My mother in law I have also been very blessed with. She was another constant for me and my two young children who were suddenly left without a daddy. But she had also lost her son who was my husband. So she was battling her own grief as well as trying to help me battle my own. There are all different types of loss as I mentioned earlier, I cannot imagine the loss of a child. It must be without exception one of the hardest of losses to overcome. Also my sister who lives in California was wonderful too and her husband. In the beginning of a bereavement, some like myself just want to draw the curtains and shut out the world. I even resented the morning light. Another day to get through. To endure. To feel my pain of loss all over again. I loved the night. At least I could get some degree of oblivion to block out the pain of my grief. However short that reprieve would be. My nights were mainly filled with anxiety and sleeplessness. So whatever reprieve I got was brief and unreplenishing.

That is what grief does. It is extremely disruptive in every area of your life. Anyone reading this will vouch for that fact. Your eating pattern also becomes disruptive. Daily routine goes out the window so to speak. Your energy levels crash through the floor and your zest and interest for life and anything related to living is lack lustre and pointless. I became like a lot of people who have a huge shock trust upon them. I acted like I was moving around in some 'robotic mode.' I was merely functioning but certainly far from living. I got up. Did what I had to do and when I could, I curled up under the covers and closed the curtains. I was unable to deal with the mounting emotions that were facing me from all sides. I did not have the tools to cope with something I had never experienced before. My energy levels had fallen to their lowest ever and I lost interest in myself and my life seemed over. Apathy was my constant emotion. That was the lowest time in my life. When you think your life is just taking up a space and feeling like a 'lost child in a large department store who has lost their mother.' That was how I was feeling most of the time. How had this happened to me? How had my life gone from one of great happiness and contentment to one of desolation and emptiness? The two extremes were intense in their differences. With a sudden death too there is no warning, no preparation, nowhere to turn. It is utter chaos. Internal and external bleakness. This is the most venerable point in a person's life. This time of extreme crisis. I began back then starting to think of when my husband was alive. He would advise me that whenever you are in a dark or bleak time in your life, just to take it 'one *hour* at a time.' One day at a time is just too much for some to handle and get through. But when I started to break it down to this bite size time-frame it became a little easier to get through the day. It was hard at first but each time I did it I realised that it was a manageable concept.

Try it yourself whenever you are in any kind of crisis – it works.! Another key saying which helped me a lot and you can try this too is to say 'And this too WILL pass ....' Because it WILL. No matter how dreadful a situation it will either pass or improve or even disappear depending on the nature of the problem. I know with bereavement the problem will not fully disappear, in so far as the person will not be coming back to this life. But you will get stronger and learn new coping skills to help lessen the loss and gain strength to move forward to a *different life*. Situations can also turn a corner or just plain disappear. They are all lessons to help us grow and in time become stronger. And yes they can be extremely hard lessons to deal with. But we can be a beacon for others who may encounter a similar adversity in their own lives. If they see how far you have come and are overcoming the obstacles in your life they will be inspired to do the same. At least they can see that there is hope. That the light at the end of a tunnel is not a fast approaching train heading in your direction. It is the light of hope and awakening to bring you to where you a *meant* to be. As I said earlier on, I don't think I ever would have written a book. Yes, at the back of my mind I always wanted to write, but I never really knew what it was I wanted to write about until five years after my husband died. It took this devastating life event to lead me to begin writing. And it feels so natural and right and something that I was strongly compelled to do. I hope by my writing my account of what happened to me and how I learned to cope and build myself back up again, that it will help those of you who are in the midst of adversity. There is hope. You will smile again. You will even laugh in time. I too was told this at the beginning. But when we are in the midst of dispair we are unable to believe that we will ever experience any degree of future joy.

What was there to smile about anyway. The life I knew and loved was gone. But a new one awaited a little way off and my journey has now begun to enrich my existence. I am starting to *live* again. And if I said that I never had a sad moment or day for that matter, I would be lying. Of course I do. I am only human. I still miss the life I had. The 'what ifs' and the 'if only he could see this'. We all have them. The person will always be there. But now I can say for sure that they are not only there with us in our hearts, but also with us in a non physical way. Looking over us and guiding us with inspiring thoughts froms where they are. I remember recently another dream I had of my husband and he told me that he would: *'be watching over me from across the Stars '*.

We as human beings still do not know where it is our Spirit goes to when our physical bodies die. But who knows in time and with the advancements of science we will be closer to finding out the greatest mystery of all time. Where do we go because we do go somewhere. I know we do. Because of all the communications I have received from mainly my husband, and also my father. With all the synchronicities which I have encountered, and all the Spiritual Teachers who have come into my life. This has and is happening for a reason. I am not asking anyone to believe or disbelieve what I have written, but to merely *accept* what has happened to me. I hope I have made what has touched my life as interesting and intriguing as I have found the events to be. It is the great unknown. Perhaps we are not meant to fully understand what and where we go. It certainly is beyond our human understanding at this point in time. Maybe we will be shown the way soon. Enlightenment can come in all kinds of different ways. We need to be vigilant to the signs and have our minds open and receptive to the incredible possibilities that are all around us but just not visible to the naked eye.

Again these *signs* can come mainly to us in the form of dreams. This was where I received my communications and guidance from. At first I thought they were just dreams. But the nature of these *dreams* were different from the normal ones I was used to having. The clarity and the whole dynamic of the dream was totally unlike any other I had experience of. As I began having more of these I realised that they were a channel of communication from the 'Other Side.' Some were clearer than others. But I found myself interacting within some of them. Lucid dreams these were. I was aware that I was *dreaming* and where my body was, but I was somewhere else. I was separate from the body. And it was not like an out of body experience as I could not see my body but at the same time I was no longer part of or connected to the physical part of who *I* was. Edgar Allen Poe once said the following : *Is all that we see or seem is but a dream within a dream?"* Dreams in themselves can seem SO real at times. We can see, feel, think, experience different emotions and sensations, and interact with other people known or not to us, all at the same time. Dreams are the brain's way of coping with daily information it receives. It occurs during the second cycle of sleep called rapid eye movement or REM for short. Interestingly enough it is during this second stage of sleep that there is more brain activity then when we are awake. This can be seen during MRI Scans. We do not always remember a dream but this does not say that we did not have a dream. We all dream every night. It could be that it helps our brains to process more efficiently when other bodily funcions are not active. Thomas Moore calls dreams "the royal road to the soul" and claimed that "it is impossible to care for the soul and live at the same time in unconsciousness." Within dreams the connection can be made between what is occurring in the body, our inner self and intuition. Via the dream process it can help us to learn what may be important in creating a situation we would like to happen. Again the signs are there and if we are tuned in enough we will hopefully be able to see these and interpret their meaning and message.

The ancient Greeks put a lot of emphasis on dreams. They would send the sick to temples called *Asclepieions* to be cured. In these temples, dreams would be incubated and used as part of the healing process. These dreams were also used to predict the future. The notion that dreams could predict the future was a big part of both Greek and Roman religion. Predicting the future through dream interpretation is sometimes called *oneiromancy*. This comes from the Greek word *oneiros* which means to dream and is a form of divination. Also in ancient Eqypt, the priest were interpreters of dreams, and these can still be seen in the hieroglyphics on some of the temple walls. In both the Old and the New Testament, dreams were often referred to as a way in which mortals communicated with God. In the New Testament, the Magi were warned to avoid King Herod (Matthes 2:12), and Paul was directed to travel to Macedonia (Acts 16:9 – 10) through a dream. In (Genesis 37:5) of the Revised standard Version of the Bible. Joseph dreamed an omen of his future success, and Jacob dreamed of a ladder to heaven where God spoke to him from the top (Genesis 28:12 – 17)

We too may be able to glimpse images given by our dreams of a future event or circumstance which has not yet happened. My own Spiritual development grew mainly as a result of my own dreams. We do not always have to look without to get answers. Some of our life's dilemas are sorted from *within*. I am not saying that everything we dream about there is a message. Some of our dreams are so convoluted that there is no reason or logic apparently to them and they can be impossible to decipher. However, although fragmented and disjointed there can be meaning and information which could be helpful in our lives. I suppose it takes a lot of practice to interpret our dreams and quite a bit of dedication. But I believe it can be worth it in the end. There can be a strong judgement in both the sleeping and waking dream which can help you become conscious of inner motivations. Action can only be taken if awareness is there. The technique of 'Active Imagining' can also prove most enlightening with regard to unlocking the mystery of the unconscious material hidden within a dream. Sharing your dream with others is an interesting interaction. When another's interpretation and view point could give another perspective and new meaning to the dream. It is no harm sharing if you feel comfortable doing so. Particularly if you really feel the need to understand what your dream is trying to convey. Family and good friends are usually helpful in doing this with and for you. If you would like to take it further and to a higher level, there are many books on dreams and workshops if this is what you would like to try and develop. Determination is the key to what feels comfortable for you. A group scenario is not for everyone. Some would just prefer a one to one. It is worth noting that when you interpret your dream to do so in relation to the rest of your present life and what is currently going on at that particular time. Jung thought that dream work was essentially a theatre in which the dreamer is the scene, the actor, producer, author, and the audience. Interesting concept. Would you agree ? Ones personality can affect symbols and the interpretation of symbols in dreams. For example whether or not you are religious and which religion you are can all have an effect on how you see your dreams to be. They can have a big influence. Personality traits such as being self-confident, anxious, possesive, perfectionist, and so on are all going to affect how you interpret the dream theme and its pattern. Also how you are feeling emotionally at the time of dreaming. Your state of mind could help with your understanding of your waking world and behaviours as well as yielding more from your dreams. They can reveal patterns within your life which are at the unconscious level to the waking mind. Our waking mind can only be objective to what is going on around it.

Dreaming is the link between the conscious and unconscious in relation to communicating with one another. Carl Jung, believed that dreams have a 'self-regulatory aspect in that they maintained the individual's balance and harmony.' He also believed that dreams 'integrated both the conscious with the unconscious.' Our dreams can often help us to problem solve what is currently happening in our lives and can at times give us solutions. It may also be a junk filter for information which is useless taken during the previous day. The Austrian psychiatrist Signumd Freud claimed that dreams were 'wish fulfilling, though this may not be apparent at first.' He also thought that 'dreams might be a projection of one's fears based on past conditioning.' Philosopher Bertrand Russell (1872 – 1970) said, "I do not believe that I am now dreaming, but I cannot prove that I am not." Some people do have recurring dreams. There may be a hidden message in this. Some area of your life which needs exploring or reconnecting to something important. They can be very fragmented and disjointed. But there can be clues within these fragments like joining a jigsaw puzzle together and eventually seeing a picture emerge to give illumination to a need or situation we are dealing with.

Because of my own amazing dreams just in the last five years I have quite an avid interest in this field. But the only difference with what I experienced was the fact that they were used as a *channel* for communication directly to me from both my father and mainly from my husband. Before this happened I was rather oblivious to the nature and structure of dreams and what their significance or substance might be. Prior to these communications, for me dreams were just dreams. And that was that. But I can now say without a shadow of a doubt that what I experienced was real and full of conviction. Because one has no *tangible* proof of producing a dream you will just have to accept my word. But there was solid guidance in those dreams. Some others had wonderful touches of comfort and consolation. In my previous dream where my husband told me that he would like me to go to the States was the start of my whole Spiritual journey. How little did I know then where it was to take me. My whole life has become more enriched and motivated as a result. I feel I have found my path. As a result of what has happened to me I am now finding that people are beginning to confide in me and telling me their life story in some cases. I can now see the vulnerability in others because I had it for so long within myself. So it is easily recognised. And I love to help when I can for whatever that is. There is such joy and a sense of achievement knowing you can help another. At least I can say that our Loved ones do continue on but very near by. They are never far away. We are being guided every step of the way. And for those of you who have lost a loved one and have not had a dream about them, what I would like to say is "Not *Yet.*" Yet being the operative word. When the time is right and you become more open, the chances of having that 'special dream' where you are some where else with the person who has passed will be well worth the wait. I can certainly say that with conviction. I can also say that I have been very blessed and privileged to have had so many 'meetings' in the dream state. I know some people who have loved deeply and forever with a significant other, and who have not had even one similar dream as I have had. I do not have the answers to why it is some of us do and some of us do not. And for those of you who have not had this dream connection, it can be difficult to relate to those of us who have. Because it has not been your experience. Perhaps you may get different signs from other areas in your lives. Flickering lights can be a common one. Objects which meant a lot to the deceased can suddenly appear in a place where you know it had not been there before. And this has not happened to me *yet.* But I know it has happened to others. But I will not dispute this just because I have not encountered it in my own reality. I am open and willing to receive all that I can. Everything seems to happen in its own good time. When and where it is meant to happen. And when we are at different times in our lives. We have to start to think outside of the box. To *see* and *listen* outside of the five senses. Not to be too judgemental or use too much logic for areas which we know little about. Just to accept that there is much more to what we can physically see around us. Again I use the analogy of the microwave, and electromagnetic waves, they are all around us. We just cannot *see* them. And yes they do not take up any space. And this is what I feel is the same with the spirit world and spirituality. It is all around us too. But the only difference is that we as yet do not have any measuring device in which to measure all of the activity. Yes we can see Orbs on digital cameras and capture images which we cannot fully explain, but these are just glimpses, the tip of the Iceberg.

Tape Recorders can sometimes detect sounds from paranormal events which cannot be heard with the human ear. EVP stands for Electronic Voice Phenomena. Or ITC short for Instrumental transcommunication. This term also includes communication via telephones, and television, computers and so forth. Laser Infrared Thermometer can detect Cold Spots which are also associated with paranormal activity. There is a very good one called the Pisto-grip meter which has a laser pointer for pinpoint accuracy. This will measure temperatures from 0 degrees up to 600 degrees at a safe distance. It also takes instant readings by simply pushing the trigger and has a back lighted display for viewing in dark locations. Then there is the Gauss Master/EMF Meter. EMF meters can detect either magnetic, electric or both types of fields together. The meter offers an easy to read analog scale, a unique built in audio signal and an auto shut off switch when not picking up energy changes. It is hand held, light and easy to use in both light and dark locations. Electric fields are measured in volts per metre (V/m) and magnetic fields usually in milliGauss (mg) or nanoTesla (nT). A compass can sometimes be an indicator of paranormal activity if it malfunctions. Interestingly enough the one common factor when activity is present of this nature is the frequency of battery life loosing power very quickly. Battery draining. But in relation to dreams it is not possible to 'capture' a dream. REM can physically show you that a person is dreaming and an MRI can show which areas of the brain are active when the subject is dreaming. But the dream *content* is not visible in any reading. Only when the person awakens is when the dream can be related verbally. So for now we just have to accept these dreams for what they are. There are no limits to the human mind's ability to generate an infinite abundance of dreams. And nobody knows exactly why we dream. It can unlock the hidden part of ourselves. By taking heed of our dreams we can lead more fulfilled lives. They give us access to that part of the mind that has intuitive knowledge of our past, present, and our future. I would like to include here a beautiful poem I read recently by Tracy Renee Shierling:

I wonder if I dreamed of you -
if you would appear?

To make my nights full of love,
and always hold me near.

I wonder if I thought of you-
if you would feel it in your Soul?
Like two Spirits in the Universe,
who always seem to know.

Even if the stars went black
and the sun were to shine no more,
They could find their way to each other,
no matter how far the shore.

Safely in each other's arms,
to bid the rest of time,
Finding Eternal Love
so many seek to find.

Caring for each other
through the worst of storms
Leaning on the arms of Love
and never need anymore.

This is how I feel for you,
I've know it all along -
My world, my heart, My Soul!
Tracy Renee Shierling.

Chapter 13

WHISPERS FROM BEYOND

"When I let go of what I am,

I become what I might be."

Lao Tsu.

In writing this work I have noticed that when I tell people what I am writing about they are keen to tell me their own experiences which they also found to be intriguing . In relation to the paranormal some prefer to keep their identities anonymous for fear of appearing off centre or just not credible. So for this purpose the following account which I heard recently I will call this gentleman *John* not his real name. Myself and John as I mentioned were talking about the subject matter of my book. And he began saying that he had also had some interesting things happen in his own life which he was unable to apply logic or justification to. He also said that he only told a very few for fear of being ridiculed or just loosing credibility with his colleagues. I of course was extremely interested and asked him if he could share some of these accounts with me and if I could mention them. He said yes and began to tell me he worked as a fireman with the Dublin Fire Brigade when he was younger. He no longer worked in the profession due to an injury. A good many years before when he was a young fireman around the nineties, a call came into the station that there was a fire in an old folks home in Dublin. When they eventually arrived there was alot of smoke as the fire had started in the kitchen so this had spread very rapidly. His colleagues and John entered the building and they were wearing their fire apparatus and breathing masks along with oxygen. He told me that the particular corridor which he went up to was where patients with dementia stayed. The rooms they were in had doors which could only be opened from the outside. So they were unable to open from the inside. Anyway he said this area was full of thick dense black smoke. Visibility was zero he went on to say. "We were trained in a situation like this upon entering a smoked filled room to feel our way along the walls so we would be able to feel our way back out of the room to avoid any disorientation. There were a few beds in that room and I wanted to make sure that there was nobody under any of the beds so this was what I was concerning myself with. But only moments after entering this room the door shut behind me and bearing in mind that this was only a one way system of opening.

I found myself locked into this area with no way out. It was pitch black and thick black smoke was everywhere. I was completely alone. To conserve my oxygen supply, I lay on the floor in the foetal position and thought I was going to die. I was hoping my colleagues would open the door and realise I was in there but the minutes went by with no activity. This area was also sound proof so that the other patients would not be disturbed by any noise. It seemed like an hour. I only had about ten minutes of my oxygen supply left and was trying not to hyperventilate. Bearing in mind I had fire clothing on which was very heavy and also my breathing apparatus and head gear. I was lying very still when all of a sudden from the *inside* of my clothing I felt a strong hand grasp my shoulder and a voice just at my ear saying "You will be O.K." It was real I felt that grip. My uniform was too thick to feel any kind of grip from the outside but this came from inside my jacket. Then moments later the door to the room I was locked into flew open and my colleagues came in illuminating the room from the corridor beyond. Both relief and disbelief filled my conscious mind. Relief that I was going to live and disbelief at what had just happened to me before the door was opened from the outside by my colleagues. It sent chills up and down my spine and still does to this day when I relate what happened to me in that room all those years ago. There was a presence with me that night. And it was there to reassure me that I would get out . I would live. I felt the touch and I heard the voice gentle like a whisper". Another time also when

I was a young fire fighter another call came in to the station. There was alot of scurrying about the place. Some of the crew descended by the pole. Being very young and full of energy I decided to go down via the stairs. This was in Buckingham Street. There was a few flights of stairs and the landings in between. Everyone had to leave and I was surprised to see two fire fighters standing on the landing below where it was I was descending. I noticed that they were dressed in the old fashioned uniform of decades before but did not particularly pay much attention to this. I shouted down to them that everyone had to leave. But they ignored me and went into the room which they had been standing outside. When I got down to their level I entered the room they had just entered in to discover that the room was empty. This completely puzzled me but it was only later that a few others told me they had also seen these two figures on that exact landing and entering the same room to also find them gone". I cannot explain it but I know what I saw and it has always intrigued me". I thanked him for sharing these enlightening and amazing experiences with me. He was glad to talk to someone who would not judge or criticise but to listen and just accept. We said our goodbyes and I was happy to be able to relate here what he was kind enough to share and we went our separate ways. It certainly is 'food for thought', again a testimony to us to know that there is so much more going on around us that we still do not have full knowledge of. We should be respectful and open to the mysteries that are around us and privileged if they can touch some of us.

There have been many speculations as to how these fascinating events can occur and touch our physical dimensional world of the five senses. We as people in general feel comfortable only talking about the tangible and what we can see and sense around us. But everything around us which is solid is not as solid as it appears. We now know that atoms are 99.999999999% empty space. That is empty of matter. Some physicists working in this area are showing that the phenomena we now call the 'paranormal' are consistent with the laws of science at the subatomic level.

The world we think of as solid is in fact energy vibrating at different wave lengths. And since we can only see a tiny fraction of those frequencies there is plenty of room for perhaps another dimension on a different frequency to enter. And because of Quantum physics, we now know that subatomic particles - electrons, protons, and neutrons, are made up of energy. I know when I *feel my husband's* presence around me it is a feeling of *energy*. It is rather like the sensation of having static electricity touching me. And instantly his memory is there very strongly at the same time I experience this physical sensation. Sometimes it is stronger than at other times. But real none the less. It is like our consciousness. It is not a tangible 'object'. But we all have it. It is real. It cannot be argued against. There should not be any reason why we cannot have consciousness without necessarily having matter. But there is so much evidence for survival after physical death. More so than the other way around. Although the sceptics would rather think differently. They are still not able to disprove the events and personal experiences of people world wide who have gone through such incidents like near death experiences or out of body events. They cannot or will not think outside of the box and just dismiss these as imagination or some kind of delusion. But it is crucial if we are to progress in the further understanding of this area, that having an open mind is paramount to being able to establish new facts and gaining more evidence for a higher understanding. We owe it to ourselves. At the very least to those who want to know more.

Every person has the right to explore without prejudice. Professor Fred Alan Wolfe talks about the Soul. He says "The question is: "Is the Soul a thing can we prove it's existence. Is it an object. It is not an noun it is a verb. The Soul is a process and because it is a process it has a consciousness and is alive. To understand life and consciousness without a tangible material that is where a lot of people have difficulty. How can anything be conscious and alive if there is no matter there". He continues to say "There has to be something before even matter appeared according to my understanding of quantum physics". What

Professor Wolfe said is something we should all think about and try to delve more deeply. There are more of us who have glimpsed interesting and unusual events which they could not explain. More people than you would think. But because there is no effective language to explain everything they keep it to themselves. I think by sharing and exchanging our encounters with one another will dispel any sense of fear and apathy for the future in the area of the paranormal. It was only last year I was thinking of going somewhere with my two children for a short holiday but had no destination in mind. Around that time, again I had a contact from my husband through a dream. He told me that Malta would be a good venue for us and in my dream, I found myself *flying* over Maltese houses from above looking down and seeing the old rustic roofs below. The many small houses clustered together and I could also see some of its countryside. He showed me this but I could not see him. I only felt his presence and heard his voice as I was seeing for myself the picturesque scene below as I passed above as if I was flying. Again I am unable to explain this but I now know where I will take my next family trip!

At least I continue to know that I am being guided every step of the way. That is not to say that I still have obstacles and decisions which I have to make but I know when I make them that they are the *right* ones for me. That bond, that connection of love and trust we have with our loved ones in this life is never broken just because they leave us physically. They can perhaps do even more for us from where it is they now are. And is this not a wonderful thing to know and a marvellous consolation to feel? We will always miss the vacant space, the return of the verbal reply, all the interactions we were used to and loved when they were alive. It is only those privileged few who have the gift to be able to communicate with those who have transitioned like mediums who can continue to interact. But for the rest of us, they do and will find their own ways of communicating with and letting us know that they are near and have not left our lives completely. And it is this awareness which has brought about a new enlightenment in my own life. As I mentioned before, I had my first amazing encounter when my daughter was only fifteen months old. Then since loosing my husband five and a half years ago that I have received more guiding communications. And also one from my father who passed on only a year before I lost my husband. I never particularly payed much attention to this side of life. I cannot say either that I had a huge interest in spirituality, I was just like everyone else in the main. But now since all that has happened I feel compelled to share my encounters and spread what I have learned and experienced.

Chapter 14
SENSING THE FUTURE

We have to appreciate the darkness
Because that is how we can see the stars.

I would like to talk a little here on the subject of premonition and precognition. These are not the same as predictions. A prediction is a forecast about the way things will happen in the future. People can forecast on anything really which they feel they have a good knowledge of. And with their expertise and experience they feel qualified to make a particular judgement either way in relation to an outcome or event happening. But premonition is a *feeling* or hunch that something which has no ground for tangible evidence or proof of an outcome happening will occur. They are usually sense oriented, and can be accompanied by feelings such as acute anxiety, a feeling of a vague discontentment that something is about to happen. It does not always have to have a negative connotation or outcome, but most premonitions which people encounter do seem to be more of a negative nature. It can also be said that something in 'one's gut' just does not feel right. These feelings can happen before events like car accidents, deciding not to take a particular flight, taking a later train, deaths, and other emotionally heightened events. This phenomenon has these global characteristics reported by those who experience these feelings. Some people may even experience visual and/ or auditory hallucinations prior to an event. These two, both premonitions and precognitions are usually classified in the same field but there is a slight difference. Premonition usually is felt within the senses and the sixth sense being the dominant for many. It can be accompanied with feelings of depression and just an overall mood of physical unease. There is also no ground for feeling like this or any reason which the person can put their finger on so to speak. Just the *sense* that something is not right or impending change in one's circumstances. This could also apply to a close loved one who they may be feeling this orientation towards.

Precognition can be said that it is more precise usually involving dreams or visions of the particular event which has not yet occurred. There can be no basis for these *dreams* or *feelings*. They are what they are. There can be a fuzzy line between these two phenomenon's. There are more details in precognition a lot of the time. Precognitive or veridical dreams are dreams which coincide with future events, or apparently unknowable present realities to give evidence that an event is going to occur. There can also be a time frame given within these dreams or visions. Some might say that premonition is a type of prophecy giving a foreboding or a preparation for a warning of some future event. Perhaps the person could be picking up signals mainly subconscious influences or inferences from an actual event or fact. There are no grounds for premonitions. But they cannot be discarded either. They are not tangible so there can be no substance to grab hold of. Premonitions which occur in the waking state are more dominant than those which occur in dreams. They can heighten our intuition and give us warnings. Some of these are not strong enough to effect us on a conscious level. They usually only register subconsciously. If they happen several times we usually remember and they can then influence us consciously. But this does not happen all the time. When we do become aware of these they can effect a change or an alteration in our plans without us knowing why. I had such a *feeling* the year before my husband died. The first of these would have been about a year prior to his passing. We had been on a week's holiday down in Kilkenny and I was just browsing through a newspaper when I came onto the houses for sale page. I had no intention of moving nor had my husband. His work was up in Dublin and we were happy where we were. But as I looked at this particular house it was so splendid that I thought it would be no harm at least to go and have a look at it. It was only a forty minute drive from where we were staying and if nothing else we could enjoy the surrounding scenery which accompanied our trip. The house itself was down in Tipperary and it was set on a few acres of land and it had a beautiful spacious front garden with a long drive up to the entrance. It was a splendid looking building built around the turn of the century. We could never afford anything equivalent to this in Dublin and we were taken by it immediately. The rooms were spectacular with stunning coving and mahogany floors and doors. The plaster work on the ceilings was magnificent. I could go on and on. It was our 'dream house'.

My husband was intrigued as I was why it was still on the market and at such a great price. It would have cost us the same in mortgage repayments as our own house did back up in Dublin but this was a mansion in comparison. My husband was trying to do mental calculations as to how he would be able to work and live down there and the logistics of maintaining a practical arrangement to facilitate a potential move. But I must say much and all as I loved this house there was a niggling feeling of disquiet I could not quite explain. The feeling was one of quiet dread. I know it sounds extreme but that was what I was picking up the whole time I was going around the rooms of this house. We decided to pay another visit at a later stage and bring along some family members to show them this house. They were also taken over by its stature and magnificence. I despite myself still had this nagging feeling of quiet despondency. There were many 'What ifs' going around in my head. And strangely enough the main one was 'What if anything happened to my husband and I was left down here alone with our two young children and knowing nobody and feeling so isolated'? I could not shake it off. What would happen to my husband? He was a very young and healthy man. Why should I be feeling like this? But I *did*......I even remembered jokingly saying to my husband that it would be dreadful to be alone down here if anything happened to him. And also at that time I was not able to drive. If the children got sick or if anything were to happen the feeling of isolation would be unbearable. But luckily for me I listened to my intuition and the premonition I had was that my husband was *not* going to be around. For some reason this was the overriding feeling all the time. He *would not* be around to enjoy this new home.

I started putting obstacles and making excuses for why it would not be feasible to move down here from Dublin and leave everything we knew behind us. I think now looking back he was very disappointed as he truly had fallen in love with our new potential home. In the end he began to realise that perhaps it would not be a good idea and reluctantly agreed not to progress any further. And a year later he was dead. Some would say it was a coincidence. But I certainly had no grounds whatsoever on which to base my feelings at that time. He was in apparently good health and still young. Why should I feel any different ? Why was I feeling like this ? But I did. And if it was a premonition well I gave in to the early intuitive warnings I was feeling inside and acted upon them. And I was so glad I did. The function of premonition is not fully known. Some people have them and some do not. But I do believe that we do all have them. But it is just that some people are more open and prone to having a psychic affiliation or suggestion. I was always very intuitive even as a child. And yes I would regard myself to being psychic and having a heightened awareness to atmospheres around me and picking up signals which others would not be aware of. Unbeknown to myself in less than a year I would be having more of these premonitions regarding my husband shortly before his death. My husband was one of life's 'Beautiful Souls'. He just exuded kindness and sunshine wherever he went. He also had that rare ability to touch a person deep within their being and make them feel blessed and happy to be alive just from being in his company. I think it is a rare quality to have. But you know when you are in the company of those who have it. They make you feel special. And we are all special. Each one of us. And we all want to feel validated as human beings. But to be made *feel* even *more* special than you are is a gift only a few have. My husband was not a rich man by any means in the monetary sense that is. But I can honestly say that he had the richest life and the richest outlook on life which I have ever encountered. He would say things like "Instead of looking at what we do not have, look at what we *do* have and to appreciate everything". He was not just talking about physical possessions like items in our homes or investments or money. He was talking also about our functioning abilities within our own bodies. Our sight. Our hearing. The fact that we can walk and run and jump those of us lucky to be able to do all that. He would say "We should get down on our knees in gratitude because we can stand up and walk". Things that we all take for granted, until we loose anyone of them. And yes we have more blessings around us than not, and to see this abundance and give thanks for what we have and what we are able to do.

He was a Music Teacher by profession. The Piano being his instrument of choice and had many students who stayed with him from little children up to grown adults. Anyone who remembers the old black and white movie 'Goodbye Mr. Chips' starring Robert Donat and Greer Garson in 1939 and directed by Sam Wood could relate to the type of character my husband was, and how he interacted with his students. He had a genuine love for each one of them and they loved him back as a respected teacher and friend. There is a line in this lovely film when someone interviewing the character Mr. Chips in the movie and he said to him what a pity it was that he did not have any children. And he replied "But I had *hundreds* of children", referring to all his students who adored him. In the film Mr. Chips is an old and dying 83 year old man. My husband was only 43 when he died, but they shared so many many similarities. I do believe he would have been the very same as the old character in the movie if he had lived another forty or so years. But I did mention this at his memorial that he was like "The 'Mr. Chips of the 'Music World". I only feel it fair to give a brief mention of my husband here in this book. He was one of the main reasons and inspirations for me in writing this. And he would have been delighted that I have done so. For his memory and for his family, but also to hopefully help others suffering the torture of bereavement and getting hope and consolation from my own spiritual experiences. And how they have helped me on the path to recovery and hope. But when he died and at the funeral mass it was evident and apparent to all present the warmth and love and profound impact his life had had on all who had been touched by his presence no matter how brief that might have been. One of his students a retired dentist thought we lead a very quiet live which we did. And could not believe the hundreds of people who turned out to say their fairwells. He said "It was like the Pope had died there were so many people there." And yes it was a testimony to the way he lived his life and all the people he loved to help and inspire and cultivate their fullest potential.

His aura was expansive and you were drawn in – very happily so. But two weeks before his passing I was beginning to feel these feelings of dread. A foreboding that he would just be gone not present in our life any more. There was nothing for me to validate these feelings. Absolutely nothing at all. But they were there. Niggling at the back of my mind. I tried to ignore them. Dismissing them as fearful notions of an possible impending loss without any grounding. He was young and healthy *I thought*. But unbeknowns to myself, his family and friends and even his doctor he was not as well as one might have thought. But hindsight is a great thing. Isn't it? Looking back there were indeed signs which I could identify that there may have been something wrong with his health. He was complaining alot of extreme fatigue and weariness not fitting with someone of his age and life style. Yes he had been very busy preparing for a Solo Concert and teaching. But all these did not correspond to how he was slowing down. I suppose it started very gradually. Subtle signs. Nothing extreme. Why worry. We all get tired don't we? But two weeks before he died he would go upstairs for a rest before leaving for work and would fall asleep and would not be energized by this. I put it down to stress and long hours of preparation on his part. However, the first of three of my *premonitions* or foreboding I was feeling started very simply one morning. I was waving him goodbye at the door and watching him get into his car. I began thinking *"What if he was no longer here...."* I quickly dismissed this silly thought and went on with my day. But a few days later I had the same feeling again. And this time I was watching him put his key into the door of his mother's house as I waited for him in the car outside. I just got this feeling again which came over me *"What if he was no longer here, what would life be like without him"?* But it was a more intense feeling and one even as I tried to ignore and push away, the feeling of impending loss was becoming more evident.

Chapter 15
THE MAGIC OF AURAS

Inever mentioned my feelings of foreboding in relation to an impending occurrence. There was no relevance to my feelings. He most likely would have laughed them off as one of those thoughts which are without logic or reason and not to be holding on to something which could be upsetting. But one week later, actually it was the weekend in which he was performing his solo piano concert in Airfield House in Stillorgan in South Dublin, I received the strongest sensation of his *moving on*. It was at the end of the second night of his recital as people were coming up to congratulate and greet him. I was waiting at the side of the room and was enjoying seeing the interchange of joy both on his face and on that of each one of the audience who had been entranced by the evening's entertainment. My attention was drawn suddenly and intently to the area around my husband. There was just such a stillness I was picking up like a *nothingness*. I later discovered what this might have been. Even though he was talking at that time with a friend's cousin of mine, he seemed to be in isolation by himself. There was no sense of a life force around him. And here I am talking about one's Aura. We all have one. Animals too. But my sense was that his life force was leaving his physical body and there was some kind of intangible change I was picking up. I remember back then thinking of the two previous occasions when I had those niggling feelings of the 'what ifs'. What if he was no longer here and this time I truly could not shake it off. The last person said their goodbyes and he began collecting his personal items which he had used that weekend for his recital. One of which was a lovely brass and marble candlelabra which was one of a pair. I was a little reluctant at first parting with this in case one of the brass arms got damaged or if someone would take it. We had a little disagreement about this in the beginning and I remember he said something to the effect of "You would be sorry if something happened to me and you did not give me that candlelabra." He said this in a half joking manner and had also said similar things about his possible passing if this or that would not happen. And this was completely out of character with anything he would normally say. Like all married couples we would have our little disagreements but in all the years we were together we never really had a serious row. I know he was stressed prior to his concert and this truly was his dream to accomplish this. All his hard work in the two years before the concert certainly paid off for him.

It was a resounding success and everyone present was moved with emotion. But it was these little things he would say about himself as if he was also picking up something which was bringing his own mortality to light. Again there was no reason. Perhaps we both could have been picking up unseen cues from somewhere not of this dimension and we both never said anything to one another concerning this. But to get back to the auras. We are all surrounded by this energy field or life force which has different colours within the aura of each one of us. When I was eighteen years old, I attended yoga classes with my mother for relaxation and towards the end of the course there was a class on auras and how to read one's aura. I found this fascinating and began practicing how to do this. We were told by our teacher at the time that it was easier to see a person's aura if they have a white or light background behind them. You were meant to stare a few inches above the head of the person you were looking at and you would begin to see a faint outline of their aura. With practice like a lot of things, this would get better and you would be able to see the colours within the aura. The teacher asked one of the class members if they would like to sit at the top of the room to have their aura read by the students. Then she would ask us if we were able to see anything. I remember at first finding this exercise difficult and started drifting. But it was in the *drifting* and the slight disassociation that I did begin to see something around the head of the student. It was vague and hazy at first but then I saw the faint outline of something around the edges of the head and around the body. I never saw any colour at first. But as the classes progressed the teacher became one of the subjects and she asked us if we would study her own aura and see if we could discern anything. She asked me if I saw something and I said I did. I told her that I could see the colour yellow and green. And she confirmed that these were two colours present in her aura.

I used to practice if I was sitting on a bus I would look over the heads of the people a few rows ahead of me and I would see the faint outline of the energy field above their heads. I was never able to see colours in this setting but it was an interesting exercise. Nearly on every occasion when I did this, invariably the person who I was trying to get a reading would turn around. It was like they knew they were being observed. Try it for yourself. It usually happens, they will look around. So you see I was extremely sensitive to this area having studied it briefly nearly thirty years before. I was picking up on the *lack* of energy surrounding my husband and particularly that second evening of his concert. There did not appear to be an aura or I could not make out a distinct energy around him which I was obviously used to picking up from him subconsciously. At that time I was unable to apply that logic to how I was feeling. It was so long since I had done any of this that I had actually forgotten about this and my previous interest and experience with auras. We were told back in our yoga class about the 'Kilner Screen.' This was devised by a Dr. Kilner back in 1911. He used colour as an aid to stimulating auric sight. Dr. Kilner researched the use of auric sight as an aid to diagnosing the health of his patients. He used Dicyanin screens for this. Dicyanin is a dye product of coal tar. These screens consisted of two pieces of glass with dicyanin dye sandwiched and sealed between them. He found that by using these – aura goggles, he could stimulate the ability to see the human aura. He would stare for a few minutes through these screens, at a bright light. When he looked away, he could see an aura surrounding his patients. He would then note any changes and abnormalities in their aura, and compare them with other observations taken of healthy people. This allowed him to detect disease in the very early stages, before the actual symptoms of that disease appeared. Dr. Kilner used several different coloured screens, and combinations of them. Different coloured screens showed him different aspects of layers of an aura. He also used strips of brightly illuminated, coloured cloth. He would stare at one of these strips, after preparing his eyes. By looking through one of his screens. These strips caused a phantom strip, of a different colour to appear in his gaze. These were like small windows, that could be moved around by shifting his gaze, highlighting different parts of his subject's aura. This gave him a different view of their aura, in that part. By looking through these screens at bright light, Dr. Kilner flooded his eyes with the slow auric colour of that screen (its reverse colour.) This made his eyes hypersensitive to that particular auric colour, enabling him to see that colour in his subject's aura.

Different coloured screens would allow him to see different colours in an aura. The use of the strips of colour, then enabled him to see the slow auric colour (reverse colour) of the coloured strip minus the original colour of the screen he was using – showing a small bank of an entirely different colour in the aura. This small band of colour could be moved around the patient's aura, by shifting his gaze, like a small window, highlighting the area it covered. After using these screens for several months he found that he needed to use them less and less. By continually straining to see auras with his aura goggles, he stimulated his brow centre, and mastered the visual technique needed to see the aura. He eventually gained full auric sight, which meant he did not have to use the goggles to see auras. The above information was taken from the book : Kilner, Walter John. (1965). "The Human Aura." There are different types of Auras. The Human Aura, The Main Aura, and The Etheric Aura.

The Human aura is an energy field that surrounds the human body, and reflects the subtle life energies at work within and around it. This is something like the magnetic field that surrounds a simple magnet. Like a magnetic field, the aura is generated within physical matter – but is also affected by it's surroundings. The energies flowing through the aura make us what we are and are in turn affected by our surrounding life conditions and life style. The aura reflects the activity of our organs, health, and mental activity and emotional state. It also shows disease – often long before the onset of physical symptoms. The strength and properties of an aura are determined by the amount of, and the quality of the energies flowing through it.

The Main Aura – The main human aura is banded around the body – strata like. It is like thick coloured hoops of light dropped over the person. The main colours of the aura emanate from the primary energy centres (major chakras – or psychic centres). The individual bands of colour are difficult to see, unless you have very well developed auric sight and are observing under optimum conditions.

The Etheric Aura. Close to the skin is the etheric aura. This is often called "The vitality sheath". It is seen (with auric sight) as a pale narrow band next to the skin outlining the body. This is usually no more than half an inch wide depending upon the vitality of the subject. It looks like a dense layer of pale smoke, clinging to the skin. This is the visible part of the energy body in it's contracted state. During sleep, the etheric aura expands and opens becoming larger and finer in order to absorb and store vitality within it. After sleep, the energy body contracts and forms a dense sheath surrounding the body close to the skin. This holds within it the stored energies we all need for living. During sleep the energy body recharges itself replacing the energies that have been used up. Energy Centers. The primary energy centres which are called *chakras,* are the non-physical organs of the energy body. There are at least seven primary centres and over three hundred secondary and minor centres scattered throughout the human body. All together, they form a complex network of non-physical energy components. These are all joined together by interconnecting pathways, or *meridians*

These centres and their interconnecting pathways (meridians) were charted by the Chinese, and other Eastern races thousands of years ago. Modern versions of these charts are all widely used today, in many types of alternative medicine and body like acupuncture and reflexology. Primary energy centres are attached to majoy internal organs, glands and nerve clusters throughout the body. There are active centres transforming and manipulating energy feeding other energy centres and taking care of life processes both physical and non physical. There are storage centre communication centres, and centres designed to absorb energy from other energy sources around us. Some energy sources. Food, water, oxygen, sunlight, planetary energy, cosmic energy, love and music. Some of these energy sources are very subtle but all are necessary for us to live a balanced life. Energy centres are invisible to the naked eye but can be felt, quite strongly, when they are active as a pulsing, thrumming sensation. When energy is consciously drawn from one centre to another through the connecting meridians, this can be felt as; A rushing water sensation, a spreading warmth, a tingling feeling, or a combination of these. Energy centres (chakras) can also be seen with auric and clairvoyant sight – as whirling vortexes of intensely coloured light. Every energy centre has important individual functions, in the energy body. It also works in conjunction with all the other major and minor centres. Each centre is an individual but integral part of the energy body. They all work together, for the good of the whole energy body, just as all the physical organs , brain, heart, liver, kidneys, glands and so on work together for the good of the whole physical body.

The energy body is extremely complex. It is in a way, similar to an electronic device. Energy flows into the electronic device and on through connecting pathways (meridians) that are etched into the circuit board. These connecting pathways (meridians) carry energy on to all it's electronic components, (chakras). Energy is continually being changed enhanced and transformed by these components; to serve a multitude of different purposes required by the device as a whole unit to function properly. A single energy centre is very much like a single electronic component. It takes in energy from the components around it and changes the value of it. It enhances this energy in various ways, transforming it into something different that is needed by the whole unit. Each energy centre (chakra) takes in the different types of energy it requires from other energy centres in the energy body and generates a completely different type of energy with a different value and colour according to what is required. The strength of each primary energy centre in any particular person depends upon that person's individual makeup: their nature, health and life style, as well as their spiritual, moral and psychic development. The energy generated by all the chakras at once, is reflected into the aura, mixing together and causing the dominant hue of the aura. This dominant hue is the part of the aura most commonly seen with auric sight.

The Seven Primary Energy Centres.
Major Chakras.

Chakras.	Location	Colour
1.Base	Base of Spine	Red
2.Spleen	Navel Area	Orange
3.Solar Plexus	Base of Sternum	Yellow
4.Heart	Centre of Chest	Green
5.Throat	Base of Throat	Blue
6.Brow	Exact centre of forehead	Violet
7.Crown	Whole top of head	Gold

Each primary is best thought of as roughly the size of your hand. So that is the technical blurb out of the way but I did include it to demonstrate how the aura is seen and read and what the different aspects and components signify. Being energy which we all are we do pick up on intangible signals from the people around us. Whether we are aware of this or not. It is a fact. You know yourself when you are being introduced to someone new, you will instantly gravitate to them or not as an individual. You are sensing their energy field as being one you feel receptive to, or the opposite a feeling of being repelled. You have heard the saying before when someone might have said "I instantly *clicked* with him or her." We can all say we have felt this from time to time Or on the other hand, there might have been something about the person which made you feel slightly uncomfortable. Just not feeling or sensing a particular affinity perhaps with the person you have just encountered. We are all giving out and receiving signals from each other and we feel their impact. They can be strong or subtle but although intangible in nature, their effect is very real indeed. It can be down to particular characteristics you sense in someone which you may not like, or want to have yourself. It works both ways. And I am not just talking about body language here.

Although that is vitally important in how we interact with each other it does not reveal our personas as much as our auras do. For example, when I took my class all those years ago and just started learning about the human aura and the different aspects of it, I remember being fascinated by the colours that are present in our auras. We all have different colours which can denote something about us and how we are as people. The following is just a brief description of what the different colours can tell about a person's traits and their personas. For example:
If someone has Red in their aura this can signify a forceful, vigorous energetic person.

Dark Red can show there is temper, nervous and domineering.
Light Red shows Impulsive, active and self-centred.
Pink is Immature.
Scarlet is Egotisitcal.
Rose is Serene.
Coral is Fearful and unhappy.
Orange in an aura shows a vital, thoughtful and considerate person.
Gold Orange is vigorous, self controlling and brave.
Brown Orange shows someone who is repressed, lacks ambition and is lazy.
Red Orange can signify someone who is egocentric.
Yellow in an aura is someone who is happy, healthy, and friendly, and who learns easily and has a quick mentality.
Lemon Yellow can show weak willed, and have an inferiority complex.
Red Yellow shows someone who is timid, shy and afraid, it is more of a ruddy yellow.
Orchid is undecided.
Indigo is a seeker after truth and who is humble.
Blue Violet – someone who has found God, but is not dedicated.
Violet is a seeker after a cause or a Religion.
Red Violet can signify sorrowful and unfulfilled.
Purple – Overbearing, and has some internal pressures.
White – The Perfect Colour. Jesus had this aura. You see this depicted in so many religious pictures.
White and Gold in an Aura shows the Ability to help others to help themselves. A Master Teacher.
Gold - Intellectual, calm and ambitious.
Blue – Contemplative and Spiritual.
Pale Blue – Struggling towards Maturity.
Medium Blue – Hard Worker, Loyal, and accomplished.
Deep Blue - Has a mission in Life..
Blue Green – Helpful and trustworthy.
Green Yellow – Deciteful.

Green - Helpful, Strong and Friendly.
Turquise – Spiritual, and has a healing ability.
Emerald Green – Healing ability particularly if it has a dash of blue.
Brown – Too earthy, carnal.
Grey – Illness.
No Colour in an Aura means Impending death.
Black – Fatal illness.

Changing Aura denotes Instability.

So that is just a brief synopsis of how the different colours can show up what our mind set is at the time. It shows our state of mind and our characteristics as people. Not to be compared to Body Language which shows how we interact with people. But the two are always present with us wherever we go and how we are perceived by the outside world. Having studied this briefly all those years ago I was perhaps a little more senstive to people's auras. This combined with a deep intuition, gave me a good insight into people. As a young child I was extremely sensitive by nature and still am to this day but not as much. These abilities have given me a little advantage when in a work or social situation. I do not have auric sight like some people but I have heard of interesting accounts of people who were able to see auras and their colours as immediate as they saw the physical person. As you have seen from the previous page some of the colours can show certain features of a person's outlook or state of mind. A terminally ill patient would probably towards the end of their physical life have a grey, black or have no colour in their aura. There was one such incident which I was told about some twenty years ago concerning one of these gifted people who had full 'Auric Sight'. This happened around the late sixties or early seventies. The date does not have much relevance to this story. But what happens within the story has relevance here and relates to the life force leaving a person's body before their actual physical death. This man was walking along a long corridor in a high rise building and at the end of the corridor were two lifts on either side of one another. He was running because he was in a hurry and wanted to catch the lift before the doors closed. However, he was not able to catch the lift in time. But he did have time to notice that the people within the elevator had a *greyness* or an *emptiness* around them and it was coming from their auras. This was noticed just before the doors were closing. He began to get a chilling and dull sensation that something dreadful was about to happen to the people he had seen only for a few brief moments. He was right. Only moments later one of the cables had snapped in the lift shaft holding the elevator and every person within had perished. This was back in the very early days when lift technology was nothing like it is today. Elevators are extremely safe today. But going back to that tragic incident. He saw no colour. Their auras were blank with nothing – an emptiness. So does this mean that just before a fatal event or sickness that the life force leaves the body *before* we physically die? It would appear so.

Because this happens all the time with people who are gravely ill. Some would say that the soul is preparing to leave and paving the way forward for the person from this life to the next? It could also be that the energy field surrounding the body has lessened due to the person's prospective demise. Something greater than us has a *knowledge* to what is about to happen in the future and it lessens the energy field surrounding the person who is about to die. There must be some intelligence behind this which makes this change.

When we are born the Soul comes in through the Lyden Centre {Second Centre}. Lyden means SEALED. When it is used positively in the body it helps both men and women. The Lyden is located down under the navel. The mind means the mind of the Soul or individual. The Lyden is the Soul of the mind. The seven spiritual centres (endocrine glands) are the pituitary gland, the pineal gland, the thyroid gland, the thymus gland, the adrenal glands, the lyden gland and finally the sexual glands. Each Spiritual centre within the body is influenced by a particular astrological force that is a physical manifestation of an afterlife realm. The Lyden which is located near the stomach, it's influence would be mysticism in astrological terms. The planet is Neptune and it is in the sixth realm. The Lyden gland is the "door" throught which the Soul may go on to higher afterlife realms. If the lyden gland is the highest spiritual center activated in a person's life, at death, their soul may dwell in the sixth afterlife realm represented physically by the planet Neptun. This is the astrological plane of mysticism. This realm is where souls have the ability to have direct experience with the Creator and perceive the Creator. These afterlife realms can be experienced when we are not active while on Earth. Our souls can explore these realms during deep sleep, meditation, hypnosis, or any other method that creates an altered state that frees the subconscious from its normal physical constraints.

The spiritual centers within our bodies are known by science to be the endocrine glands also know as *chakras* which I was talking about earlier. These are the emotional and motivational centers of the body. Our spiritual centers serve as points of contact between the spirit and the body and are the transformers of the divine spirit into physical consciousness and manifestation. Through our spiritual centers, our spiritual force finds a means of expression. It is through these spiritual centers that the physical, mental and spiritual forces all come together. These centers are the organs of perception through which we can become aware of the spirit realms in the same way that our five senses are organs of perception of the physical realm. Our spiritual centers are influenced by astrological forces that represent and correspond to the spirit realm. The highest spirit realm we can inhabit after death is determined by the highest spiritual center activated within our body by the spirtual force within.

The following is a list of the human body's spirtual centers, the astronomical influence on them, and their corresponding afterlife realms.

Gland	Location	Influence	Planet	Realm
Pituitary	eyes	strength	Jupiter	7th
Pineal	brain	mind	Mercury	2nd
Thyroid	throat	psyche	Uranus	8th
Thymus	heart	love	Venus	4th
Adrenal	Kidneys	anger	Mars	5th
Lyden	stomach	mysticism	Neptune	6th
Sex glands	groin	purification	Saturn	1st
body	testing		Earth	3rd

The above are the endocrine glands. Their location. Their influence. Their corresponding planet and the realms. Each Spiritual centre within the body is influenced by a particular astrological force that is a physical manifestation of an afterlife realm.

We know the different divisions of man's awareness to be the conscious mind (physical awareness), the subconscious mind (soul), and the superconscious mind – the (Spirit). Like the different levels of awareness, we also see our lives as being divided into the physical, the mental, and the spiritual sectors of our full human existence. And we normally relate, react and function within these five senses. But the sixth sense is very real. It is as much a part of our daily life as the other five but it can be the most elusive. It is this sense which we can see and feel and react to without dependence on the other five senses, and without the need for any evidential knowledge or tangible information.

Chapter 16
ENERGIES AND THEIR VIBRATIONS

Cayce was a gentleman who dealt with the realms of the Afterlife and the body's connection to astrology. He had a few revelations. One of which he stated that if a soul has a spiritual ideal and desires to know it, it possesses that ideal, the soul can come to this physical realm to be tested and apply it themselves. He said by going through the experience ourselves on earth, we can realize if what we believe is true or not for ourselves. The Earth realm is good for overcoming certain weaknesses. We apply ourselves to see that those weaknesses are truly overcome. Here on earth we can learn whether we have really changed. We come to earth to assume a body of flesh and are tested in ways that only a human body can. Each one of us experience all that life has to offer. The good, the bad, the wonderful, the positive life changing events we encounter which can enrich us, and of course the devastating events which will at times touch our human existence at some stage or other. All contribute to different levels of growth and teachings. We can become empowered and infused with a deeper wisdom and a sense of growing as individuals when we can find the hidden lessons within every situation we encounter in this life. Those lessons can be hard to find and even more difficult to live through. Again bereavement is probably one of our biggest lesson in going deep within ourselves. It can be a debilitating and isolating feeling at the best of times, depending on the type of loss and how close the person was in your life before their passing. Isn't it interesting that it is nearly always the most difficult of situations which can teach us the greatest lesson? We all know the saying "Every cloud has a silver lining." But some clouds are harder to push away in order to see the sunshine.

Out of nearly every calamity comes something good or useful for our higher growth. It certainly may not appear like that at the time with any loss or upset, it may even take years to realize this. But good will eventually make its presence felt and a stronger you *will* emerge . It can be a very long process. I think I am qualified to say this. After all I went through so many calamities and adversities in my own life. If anyone had said to me what I am now saying back then, I would have said they had no notion what they were talking about. I could give a Master Class on Loss, but that would be for another book! After all I lost not one but three babies through the painful and devastating loss of miscarriage. And I *felt* each individual loss. Then several years later, our beautiful long awaited baby was born with Special Needs. Incidentally I would not change a hair on his head and love him as dearly as if he were quote on quote 'normal' And how do we define what is normal anyway. The only *normal* I know is the setting on my 'Washing Machine'! As my husband said when he was born "He is a *different* kind of Perfect. Every child has a right to walk under the sun." He was and still is perfect to me. Then my father died and the following year my young husband died leaving me with a three and a nine year old. So if I can survive these intense and devastating of life's adversities and still come out stronger in the end – well so can you. We all have this within ourselves. We are stronger than we give ourselves credit for. It is just a question of being able to tap into the best and the highest of who you are as a human being. And it is completely different for every one of us as individuals. Our coping mechanism is unique as is our outlook on life. Outlook has alot to do with our recovery. We have to heal. It takes as long as it takes. Like a sore or cut a scab forms over this and it falls off when the wound underneath has healed. There is no rushing this. It will fall off when it is good and ready.

If we rush the process and scratch the scab you only compound the problem underneath. Then the recovery time takes longer. It is the same with emotional pain. But these wounds are not visible to others as much. For me I found a good way to track my own recovery was not in the 'looking ahead' in life, but on the 'looking back' and seeing how far I have come. You should try this too for anything which has occurred to cause your life to be touched with sadness. You will realise that one day the pain is not as deep. Yes, it never fully goes away, but you do learn new ways of coping and moving on. And saying the following helped me as well; "And this too *will* pass....." and this too will pass. Because it will in its own time. The process can be long and hard. Do not let anyone tell you otherwise. But get whatever support mechanism you can which is good for you to help move you along in your healing progress. And take out the 'what ifs' from your vocabulary. 'What if this or that would have been done they would still be with us.' Or 'If I had only known I would have been there more often.' That is just another way of beating yourself up with unnecessary baggage and hardship. When those thoughts creep into your mind just face them and say out loud STOP! It will not become as powerful as time moves on. You will learn to control your thoughts for some of the time anyway. And pay attention to how your thoughts are influencing your progress. I have always been a believer that everything that happens in our life happens for a reason and for our highest good. Even when someone young passes on. I try to feel that it was their time to go. It was part of a bigger plan even before they were born. We all have a time to be born, to live, and a time to leave. There seems to be a degree of this being ordained from a higher level. We touch people with our lives and they in turn touch our own lives. Like the poem I included earlier on when a person comes into your life for a reason, a season, or a lifetime. They come and they go. We do learn whether we know it or not. Especially through loosing someone although the hardest cross it can yield the strongest lesson.

The longing and the feelings of loss will always be with us, but to try and celebrate the fact that we had them in our lives for whatever time that was. Sometimes a little shift in our thinking can bring us renewed strength and enlightment no matter how bad a situation is.

Thoughts are so very powerful and their effects can be far reaching. Again thoughts are energy. And energy effects everything around us. And within us. The first negative sign of emotional distress and persistent negative thoughts is illness and disease. Dis – ease we are not at ease with ourselves. There is a disassociation, a disconnection from ourself. I liken it to an implosion effect. When we internalize something painful for too long and do not adequately express it, it starts to eat away at the core of our being and can cause physical things like ulcers, headaches and all sorts of problems. The more the pain is pushed deep down the bigger it gets until eventually it cannot be contained. Things like emotional outbursts, panic attacks, and feelings of futility can be products of this. It is crucial to have your grief professionally managed if possible and to put the proper perspective and normality on the feelings you are having. I have now joined a support group for people like myself who have lost a significant other in their life. But it has taken me five years to be able to do this. I certainly would not have had the emotional strength to face a group of strangers and open up my inner pain. And this is not for personal validation. It is for sharing my story and listening to the other stories of people who are in pain. There are different levels of loss. But it is in the *interchange* of our experiences with one another that the feeling of isolation and not being 'the only one' is very therapeutic. In the beginning I had a 'one to one' counsellor who was inspirational and put relevance and normality to my feelings. There was consistency is these meetings. And this is important.

Find the necessary tools in moving forward which suits your particular needs at the time. It is always a bonus to have someone who not only understands what you are going through, and the steps needed for recovery. But someone who has already *been there themselves*. Greater clarity and structure can be instilled more effectively by someone who knows exactly where you are coming from. The power of empathy is huge and far reaching. The feelings of isolation are not as daunting and as crippling when conversing with another who has walked your path before. I was privileged to have had such a wonderful person who sat and listened on a weekly basis to my then chronic apathy on my life's future purpose. And now here I am six years along the path of life and writing this. If anyone had told me back then that I would be writing a book of any kind, not to mention one on healing and moving on, I would have thought they were deluded and living on another planet! Life is a constant changing process. Some would also say a 'work in progress.' Even if we stay still life constantly moves around us and brings with it new horizons and opportunities. Including the people we know. Their lives are also in a process of movement and change. Eventually we will wake up to life's possibilities of which there are many. When we feel strong and brave enough, we will be more able to venture forward and take the baby steps necessary for healing. Nobody ever said it would be easy. But with patience and setting small goals, you will emerge like the butterfly into a new type of you. Spreading your wings and taking off into new situations can be daunting for most people. But the key is to start off small. Not to have too high expectations will enable you to at least try. Get a buddy to go with you. And give yourself a certain bite size goal nothing too adventurous. And be kind to yourself. We are our own worst critics. Don't be judgmental. Allow time for inner strength to return. It will eventually.

I have included the following beautiful poem which I think is appropriate for anyone who has lost someone close and special in their lives. Enjoy!

You can shed tears that they are gone,
Or you can smile because they have lived.
You can close your eyes and pray that
they will come back,
Or you can open your eyes and see
all they have left.
Your heart can be empty because
you cannot see them,
Or you can be full of the love
you shared.
You can turn your back on tomorrow
because of yesterday.
Or you can be happy for tomorrow
because of yesterday.
You can remember them only that
they are gone.
Or you can cherish their memory
and let it live on.
You can cry and close your
mind
Be empty and turn your back,
Or you can do what they would want;
Smile, open your eyes, love
and go on .....

by David Harkins.

PART III

"The joy of a Spirit is the measure of its power."

Ninon de Lenclos

(1620 - 1705)

Chapter 17

THE SIXTH SENSE

- OUR SPIRITUAL BEACON

"Cease every joy to glimmer on my mind. But leave
oh! leave the light of Hope behind."
Thomas Campbell (1777 – 1844)

I said I had sensed and was picking up on the lack of life force around my husband's body shortly before he died. His aura was obviously changing and had changed quite dramatically during the few days before his physical passing. His mood was also more sedate and still. He spoke less and seemed a lot less animated. He would normally have been a vivacious and high energy person with a great deal of exuberance. So there was also some internal stillness within his own being. He started alluding to his father's death at the young age of only 53. The thoughts of his own mortality were becoming a bit of an issue which before then would never have entered his mind. Particularly referring to a photograph taken of himself on the night he had finished his own piano recital. It was a digital photograph of himself so he saw it instantly. The resemblance of Owen to his father in this particular photograph was quite striking and he wanted me to destroy it. Not because he disliked his father, he loved him. But because there was something about that picture which unsettled him. He could see his own mortality and he felt uneasy. The night he said this I took a second picture of my husband also a digital photograph, and there was an orb to the left of his head. Only about two to three inches away. Since his father was very much on his mind, who is to say that perhaps this orb could have been the presence of his own father who knew he would be departing this world very soon. It was a foreboding he was picking up on and I was sensing it too but I never knew the full significance of what was about to happen at that time. I soon was to experience only two short weeks later exactly what it was. It had all made sense afterwards.

Hindsight again is a great thing isn't it. It was not until several years later that I fully understood what was happening. With the grief process and being in the very early stages of bereavement, it was not possible to identify any of this at that time. Getting through a day had its own turbulence to be dealing with. I now remember thinking back to the first time when I became familiar with auras and being told that it is not just human beings who have auras. It is all living creatures. Cats, dogs, and animals of all kinds have their own auras. There was one incident I heard about where a pet owner who had the ability to see auras. This man had a cat. One day he noticed that the aura surrounding his cat which was normally quite far from it's body, had all of a sudden gone in very close to the cat. Just then the cat went to the side of the garden and got sick. It later recovered with no adverse effects but the aura or life force was weak. When we are in good health it can be quite high around our bodies, but when we are not in the full of our health, it can be closer to our bodies. I thought this was an interesting observation by the cat owner. I suppose we have all felt this with certain people we do not know. Upon entering a room a person who has a lovely or a healthy big persona for people to say things like *there was a wonderful aura about that person.* They just radiate something extra about themselves which you cannot see but can feel around them. And they do not have to be big in physical stature either. It is their energy which attracts others to them in a positive way. On the flip side if someone does not have a good energy about them or who is mean and selfish it works in the same principle. And our auras can change all the time. Depending on our moods, our health and our outlook. Our perception of ourselves and others can change the colours within our aura. We nearly all have an overall dominant colour. This is the *essence* of who we are as people and it has our main character and personality trait.

So you see there is more than just body language which can attract or repel you to different people. One can change their clothes or hair or makeup but it is not the case with the auras we carry around our bodies. There is no disguising that. It is an intrinsic part of who we are and we are continually picking up these cues all the time from everyone around us. Recently I have been drawn to this fact more so since I came to writing this book. A relative of my husband was terminally ill. She has now since passed on. I have been in to visit her on several occasions. But again on each occasion I picked up the 'stillness' around this person and with some of the other patients who were in the hospice. It is not just the case or fact that their bodies are gravely ill. Naturally their energy levels would be extremely low. But there is also the lack of substance which I picked up from around them. If I had full auric sight I would perhaps see a greyness or an emptiness which predominates in their auras. Especially if that person is about to pass over. I still do not understand the *stillness* which seems to be outside of their bodies though. Perhaps it is an extension of their energy levels beginning to change, leave, and move on. I am sure people who work with and care for hospice patients could say they have similar feelings. Nurses and health care workers who would know a hospice patient for a long time and then just prior to their passing would probably experience a tangible change around the dying patient too. Isn't it also interesting that we have heard of certain animals who will go to a certain patient only a few hours before they die. Sometimes only a matter of hours. They do say that animals are sensitives and can pick up on these changes more efficiently than we can. They can also sense if there is a presence with us or in a house. They seem to be able to see the unseen. So they too have the 'sixth sense.' And we should respect this about animals.

I believe they can teach us a lot in this life. Their psychic abilities can be astounding too. Most pets will get up and move about the house and go to the main door when their owners are about to return home. And they can be miles apart. There seems to be some telepathic communication going on. And they are so empathetic to us and our feelings. Whether we are happy, sad, angry or in grief, they will always pick up these feelings with a skillful knowledge. I remember shortly after my own husband passed I was in his mother's house and she had a little white westie called 'Shadow.' He was a lovely little fellow and would usually greet me when I called to the house and then go on his way. This was always the case with him. But when I came up to the house he never left my side. He stayed with me all the time obviously tuning into my grief and trying to give me comfort by his presence. When my extreme grief passed he did his usual greeting and continued on his way. He sensed my loss. My actions never changed but my emotional state had. He was picking up on this. We receive wonderful solace and comfort from our pets. Their unconditional love is just beautiful. They are in complete acceptance of who we are despite all our human failings. They love us despite this and it is a privilege to be touched by such integrity and sincerity. Even when we die you have heard cases of animals lying beside a grave of their master or mistress sometimes not eating and staying out in all weathers. Their loyalty goes beyond the boundaries of most human relationships. They hold the essence of what true love should be.

I had an interesting experience with a lovely little cat I had for three years called Fluffy. He really was basically a house cat and I was not able to send him out as I lived on a busy main road. So for fear of him being put in dangers way by running across our road, he became like one of the family. But on one particular day I let him out in my back garden for a little ramble and exploration. Bearing in mind he would normally only go three to four gardens either side of my house for his roaming expeditions! But on this particular occasion I remember him sitting on my kitchen roof and just chilling out in the dull winter's sun. But for some unknown reason I found myself staring at him and again wondering what it would be like not to have him anymore. As I gazed at him I was thinking what a handsome little fellow he was but he seemed more quiet then usual and for want of a better word more 'pensive'. If one can apply this to an animal. I was picking up *something* from around him which I could not fully explain. The same vibe I had experienced with my husband shortly before his passing. I thought no more about this. Continuing on with my day it was time to call him in. As I called him expecting his furry little body to dart quickly past me into the kitchen which was his usual manner of entry, but there was no sign of him. I called and called and thought to myself that perhaps he had gone further on in his travels then normal. So, I decided to wait till later knowing that he would be hungry and want his dinner. But later arrived and no cat emerged despite my tenacious attempts at persuasion in all the ways I knew he would respond to. I began to feel uneasy. Something was not right.

The day came and went and so too did the night. I was hoping with apprehensive optimism that he would be at the door the following morning. Alas still no sign and I just had this sinking feeling that all was not well. One day went by. Two and three days with no cat. Then one morning I was walking down my stairs and I got this sick sinking feeling in the pit of my stomach. I *knew* my little companion had died. Just then the door bell rang and two little girls who lived next door told my husband that our cat was dead and someone had placed his little body in a local grotto at the end of our row of houses. I was so upset. It broke my heart. I loved this little cat. And any of you who have lost a beloved pet will empathise as to how I was feeling. The loss of an animal who is your constant companion can be a hard blow to take. But I began to think back to the last time I saw him on my kitchen roof and feeling the same feeling around him that he was not going to be with me for much longer. I think that was the very first time I had acknowledgement of this from an animal. His aura was obviously changing and it was this change, this intangible aspect *about* him which I was sensing but not being fully aware as to what it was I was picking up. You see our *Senses* do not deceive us – our *judgement* does.

Now one could say that it was my instinct or intuition. And perhaps it was. But looking at him visually back then he seemed physically unchanged. He looked healthy and vibrant. But it was not his physical body, it was *something around* him. And I can only apply this to his energy field around him his aura which had changed. And this was what I *saw*. Strange to say the next day after he disappeared I had a ball on the floor of my kitchen which was well away from the door and my windows were closed. But when I opened my kitchen door from my periferal vision I could have sworn that I saw his shadow run in through the door and the ball at the far end of the room started to move. We used to play with this ball or any one he could find. I would roll the ball towards him and he would roll it back to me with his paw. He loved fun and loved to play. But again I put it down to my imagination or a trick of the light. I think I know better now.

We have all heard the stories of animals who start to stand up and go to the hall door when they sense that their owners are returning home. Our own innate intuition is a valuable asset and can be a guiding force in our daily lives. By enhancing our intuition it appears it may also enhance the emotional connection and the deep bond we have with our pets. This enhanced intuition could increase our ability for telepathic communication. Our pets can often tune into this. Both us as their owners and our pets can sense the unconditional love moving back and forth between us. This emotional tie can be very strong and makes for a bond which some of us find difficult to replicate with our fellow human beings. Animals are fully accepting of us. Despite our flaws and because of them too. If this type of love and acceptance was replicated more in our society, this world would be a much happier place to live in. Would you agree ? Animals can teach us more than we realise. We should respect and love them. They are such a gift! Animals are completely similar to us in so far as they have a life force, an energy field, an aura which surrounds their bodies as well. Our Auras which is our energy field has seven layers. The Chakras are the energy vortexes of your consciousness. When your energy system is healthy and balanced your life can transform in a very positive and good way. This in turn will release your full potential. Because your energy is basically you. So as a result when you have this positive energy around you you are transforming your reality in positive ways back into your life. Aine Belton – Matrix Shift – Change Your Energy – Change Your World says that your energy system is determining your life experience right now, for better or worse.

Any problem in your life exists as energy in your field. When you clear, heal, balance and optimize your energy system, you transform your being and your reality as a result. She says that 'You and Your Reality are inextricably linked. As within, so without! Whatever's going on 'out there' in your world relates to something going on at an energetic level. Any issue, be it scarcity, low confidence, emotional pain, a lack of success or low self-esteem etc, is a reflection of the energy patterns in your matrix. But you can transform them and that is the good news. When you clear energy blocks, discordance and lower frequency energy you also clear reflections of that disharmony that are manifesting in your life, be that in the area of love, wealth, happiness, career, relationships, happiness, well-being, and so on. Things exist as energy *before* they manifest as form. She continues by saying that problems and dysfunctions in your life, even physical 'dis-ease' in the body, exist at an energetic level first. Healing at a vibrational level not only prevents issues from showing up in your life, but can also resolve your current problems *from the inside out!* When you positively alter vibration, you positively alter EVERYTHING.

"Everything is energy and that's all there is to it...It can be no other way. This is not philosophy. This is physics." - Einstein.

When you break matter down to the smallest level, there is nothing solid at all. Energy is the very substance of life, the fabric that underpins ALL, referred to by some as 'life-force', 'chi', 'ki' 'prana', 'universal energy', 'pure consciousness', 'infinite intelligence', or 'light'. Quantum science confirms reality as energy. This energy is an intelligent force, as Max Planck, one of the founding fathers of Quantum Theory, wrote: "All matter originates and exists only by virtue of a force which brings the particles of an atom together. We must assume behind this force is the existence of a conscious and intelligent mind. This mind is the matrix of all matter." - Max Planck.

To go back briefly to the time before I lost my cat. I had nothing tangible to substantiate my *feelings* that he would not be around for much longer. But it ensued that the following day he was knocked down and killed by a car. It was only a week later that his body was discovered. So the energy in his aura was perhaps *sensing* a future event which had not yet occured in reality? Reality exists as energy before it manifests physically. Thoughts quite literally become things. Quantum science now proves you are not separate from your experience. What appears to be solid stuff out there is, in fact wavelengths of energy that respond directly to you. Reality is an infinite sea of possibilities made manifest by the energy you project upon it. When you experience the world as energy, including you and the people and situations in your life, a whole new dimension opens up. Thoughts and feelings are energy and they directly impact your energy system and body. Working with energy is not at all new. It has been harnessed in spiritual and healing practices and traditions for centuries . It is used by many reputable healing and well-being arts systems that acknowledge the human energy field and universal life force. These include, Yoga, Reiki, Acupuncture, Thai Chi, EFT, Qi Gong, and many others too. Energy also plays an acknowledged role in The Law of Attraction, Visualization, Theta Healing, Clearing and release processes. Meditation, Crystal healing, Brainwave entrainment, and Sound healing.

Positive thinking and focussing on your strengths and abilities can all help to raise your vibration and therefore change your energy. You will in turn attract more positive people and situations into your life. People will notice a good 'vibe' about you. This word of course comes from the word 'vibration'. I am sure you have noticed this yourself about the different people you interact with on a daily basis. They are giving out different *vibes* all the time. Some good some not so good. We all like to be around those who have a good 'vibration' surrounding them. Sometimes we are unable to define what it is about a particular person, but that is what it is. And we are very attracted to it. And like radio frequencies we are tuning into their subtleties all the time. We take our *energy* with us wherever we go. We can change our physical appearance but how we feel and who we really are is intrinsically manifested in the energy we carry around with us. People with a lot of charisma have this. They just exude it. And it is extremely enticing. Not to say that people who do not have charisma have poor energy - not at all. But when you get the combinations of high energy, great vibrations, *and* charisma – that can be electric! Some public figures have this and are extremely successful in what they do. Their countenace is more positive and their demeanour more convincing. They believe in themselves and fully believe in what particular path they have chosen in life. As a result they are more fruitful and competent in whatever field they choose to follow. They are a guiding force. And that force is the impact and culmination of the energy around them. Change your thoughts, change your life, change *the World*... *!* The power of one is so strong. You can change your own world for the better and those who come into contact with you in the same positive way. It is the ripple effect. It can be more far reaching then you could ever have imagined. So cast yourself with magnificence into the waters of life and make it count! It is never too late to make the change. You must change your mind set first, and then the rest will follow! As the saying goes "Be the change you want to see in the world."

I have been blessed with signs from the spirit world since the loss of my young husband and even before that. I have also been privileged to have received coherent signs as well. I am fully aware that not everyone receives signs from a loved one once they pass over. Perhaps they do and the signs may appear convoluted or vague. Or the loved one left behind may not perhaps be either open to or have recognition to the fact that they have received a sign. Some people who are more receptive to signs will have a higher chance of becoming a witness to and thus experiencing a contact. An open mind is crucial. In my own case they mainly came when I was asleep and dreaming. We detach completely from reality during sleep. We are not capable of filtering what comes into our dreams because we are not conscious. This brings me to an interesting event which only recently happened to me again in a dream. Here I can only relate my own experience, take from it what you will. But again I found it to be quite intriguing and would like to share it with you. In this dream I heard my husband's voice. And he simply said "Tomorrow I am going to give you a sign to watch out for that I will be around." And that was it. I woke up shortly afterwards and kept thinking of what the dream meant. I remember telling my daughter with excited anticipation about the dream and for her to also look for some sign which I may miss. Anyway the day came and went and nothing out of the ordinary occurred. But that evening when I was alone by myself in the living room watching the television, something made me look to the other side of the room at the wall facing the television. And there beneath one of my chairs was my son's runners. Nothing strange or out of the ordinary about that I hear you say. But before I explain what happened next let me describe these runners first. They are the ones which have the little lights inside the heel. These lights go on and off when there is pressure applied from above. You will really notice them more in the dark when the child runs or walks then these lights will go on. Or if they were thrown and pressure applied by the force of throwing the shoe. Otherwise these lights remain off. So as I was saying my attention was brought to the other side of the living room.

I remember looking at the clock near the television before I turned around and it was eight fifteen in the evening. The room was very quiet. I was lying down on my sofa and there was no vibrations or physical activity around or near the runners. When all of a sudden I noticed under this chair one of the runners which incidentally was on its side, had the lights turning on going back and forth around the base of the shoe. The lights were on for a good ten seconds and then stopped. Bearing in mind that these lights are integrated within the sole of the shoe and can only be activated with pressure from above. Well neither happened to create these lights to go on. I was incapable of giving any logical explanation as to why they began to switch on and activate themselves. There was no external stimulus or physical enducement to explain this. And instantly I was drawn back to my dream the previous night when my husband told me to look out for a sign to let me know he would be around. I had *received my sign*...And I was delighted! I remember going over to the shoe and I even tried jumping near it to create some major vibration to trigger the lights, but nothing happened. The lights in the shoe remained off and nothing would activate them. I did this several times in the days which followed and despite my efforts the shoes did not budge or light up. So explain how this could have happened. I just put two and two together and an illogical event became a little more logical. The dream plus this event occurring equalled my resulting sign. Take from it what you will. If we become more receptive to signs opening up around us it will help to heighten our level of awareness. Sometimes on occasions like this we truly have to think outside of the box. We are unable to apply logic to everything. And just accept that some things are beyond our human understanding. And I think if we take this approach to many spiritual aspects of life in general, we will be able to open up to and thus expand our minds to the wider possibilities to what is out there and beyond the five senses. Sometimes we get small indiscernible *nudges* from the other side but we decide to dismiss them as nonsense or our imagination 'playing up.'

But I truly believe if we are more objective to the unexplained and the irrational we could learn a huge lesson in our perception of Mortality. A death ends a life, but remember it never ends *a relationship.* Yes, because we live in this physical dimension it really is all we know as human beings. But if we think of ourselves as 'Spirits having a Human Experience' instead of as ' 'Human Beings with a Spirit' our perception will change wonderfully. Our shift and our paradigm will also move into a different level of consciousness and awareness and we become freer as a species. We are all here to learn a lesson or lessons. And some of these lessons can be hard and devastating ones. But we are survivors and what does not break us down – builds us up. And it does seem unfair that it is the tragedies in our life which gives us the greatest growth. But it is none the less true. It is times like these that test us as people and how we respond to the changes which we find crossing our lives. It can be the ultimate endurance test. To discover that the life you knew and loved and felt comfortable with, is no more. Your identity and focus has to shift and move in perhaps a direction which you never would have taken or expected to go in. But we are always guided and in the midst of change there is a higher power working for your highest good. And I know at the time that is the last thought in your mind, but some good will eventually come from tragedy. Even in the way people rally around you and the kindness of human nature shows its face in basic humanitarian ways. Love always finds a way.

These were the pair of runners with the integrated red lights in the heels. It was these shoes which lit up by themselves untouched by any external stimulus which my husband told me in a dream the previous night that he would send me a sign to look out for.

Chapter 18

THE BLESSINGS OF MEMORIES

"Fulfilment does not come by having dreams,
but by following them."

One place which my husband and I found to have a haunting quality to it was Celbridge Abbey in County Kildare. I remember going there with him and our two young children at the time. It would have been around Christmas of 2003, nine years ago. Not knowing it was to be the last time we would be there as a family together. It was a place with beautiful walks by a winding river surrounded by trees and foliage of various colours. Golds, copper, reds and of course a thousand shades of green! But it held such a spiritual quality about it which one could only sense and feel its touch as you walked through the old grounds filled with history and culture. It was one of '*Our Special Places*'. To mention Celbridge Abbey and not mention it's history would be remiss of me. But in brief a gentleman called Bartholomew Van Homrigh who was a Dutch merchant and a compatriot of King William of Orange. He built Celbridge Abbey shortly after 1695. He then later became Lord Mayor of Dublin in 1697. His daughter Vanessa had a relationship with Dean Jonathan Swift, author of "Gulliver's Travels." Swift and Vanessa met several times in Celbridge and had a tumultuous love affair. Henry Grattan the famous Parliamentarian, frequently visited in Celbridge Abbey and says he was richly inspired by the beauty of the walks. So inspired was he that his inspiration brought about the speech which he composed for the "Declaration of Rights" which led to the setting up of Grattan's Parliament in 1782. So as you can see the Abbey is steeped in history. But history aside there is an ethereal quality about this wonderful place. It goes beyond the physical beauty of it's vicinity. It is in the air, the atmosphere of the place. It surrounds you and you fall willingly into its grasp. As well as the enchanting surroundings and fine walks, there was a lovely little coffee shop and another centre which was selling fine Christmas trees both real and artificial. So it was into this section we finally strolled and purchased a beautiful artificial tree which I still have today. It is so life like no one believes it to be fake it is only when I tell them. Shortly after purchasing the tree and one or two other little interesting items we were later told that the grounds of the Abbey were soon to be closed to the public on the grounds of health and safety. We were very disappointed as this was an oasis of splendour so close to Dublin where you could go to detach from the fast pace of reality. Here you had 'A *feast for the eyes, and 'food for the Soul.'* What a pity not to be able to see this again for whatever length of time was genuinely very sad. But we hoped that this would not come to pass and that it would hopefully remain open for some time to come in the future. But the future did arrive and yes the Abbey Grounds did close. They have remained so ever since. And in the early years to follow after its closure my husband and I used to talk of how sad it was that it was still there, the grounds, the glory of the surrounding nature and so on but not being able to visit again made us feel a sense of loss and futility. I had to mention this background before I reveal my next unusual incident which happened to me in relation to the Abbey. Earlier on in a previous chapter I mentioned synchronicities and how they can enter into our lives. But my next story was very interesting in relation to more coincidences which began to unfold. Further confirmation that I was not alone.

Twice every year for the past three years I have been going to a fabulous Garden Centre in Celbridge called 'The Orchard'. My grief counsellor at the time and now good friend goes along with me and we make a good day of it. I have been there several times in the past, and nothing out of the ordinary in relation to my visiting has ever happened - until this one morning.... I had arranged with my friend Pat to go to the centre and she was meeting me later that particular morning. For some unknown reason the night before, I began thinking about Celbridge Abbey and how I would love to go back for a visit. And bearing in mind that it was at least seven years since I had been there. So normally it would not have entered my mind. However, I began to think how lovely it would be to be able to go back for one more time. Just to walk around the grounds even though my memories would be bitter sweet. I then spoke this thought out loud to my husband and said what I was thinking. I thought no more of it. The next morning I had everything ready to go and was awaiting my friend's arrival. All went well. She called up and we both headed to the garden centre. But when we arrived at 10.30 am that morning we noticed that everything was dark and seemed to be locked up. What was going on we wondered? So we got out of the car and walked up to a member of staff who was putting up a notice on the main entrance to the centre. What had happened was that the night before a pole which was across the road from the garden centre had been hit by a truck. The pole was badly damaged and the driver thankfully was unhurt. The electrical cables which ran from this pole gave the centre its power supply. And so they had to close up until the situation was rectified. "This has never happened before" said a member of staff. "Someone who saw what happened the previous night said it was like 'blue fireworks' coming from the pole". It had completely disabled the power supply inside and would have to be fixed. "So we are hoping to open around midday." As it was early november and quite a chilly day, they had no choice but to close their doors.

To commence business and allow the public to enter would have to be postponed. I was so disappointed as was my companion. But then she turned to me and quickly said "I know, she said, "We will go to *Celbridge Abbey* and I can park my car there and we can go and have tea until the centre opens. By the time we drive there and stay in the town and drive back hopefully all will be fixed by then." Well ......I said nothing for awhile and just looked at her and remembered thinking only a little earlier in my kitchen how I longed to go back to that beautiful place with all the special memories it held and the peace it instilled. She just looked at me as I suppose my expression must have given away some of what I was thinking. "Pat do you know I have not been to the Abbey for years since Owen died and I was only this morning speaking my thoughts out aloud to him expressing how wonderful it would be to venture back in to this incredible place - and now *this* has happened ?? Being a wonderfully spiritual person herself this did not very much surprise her. She just listened and accepted my conviction that this was no accident. It was such a synchronicity which had taken place. "Yes, she said Owen heard you and this was his way of letting you know he is still with you. This was no coincidence us finding ourselves driving on down the road and entering the old town and heading for the entrance to Celbridge Abbey.... A moment I will not forget for a long time. If the garden centre had been open I may have never entered Celbridge Abbey ever again. The day was cold but bright. With that winter sun which is low on the horizon and can cut your eyes with its brightness. We entered the car park of the old Abbey and I gazed at the place we as a family used to park our own car all those years ago. Alas, the main grounds were still closed. All I could do and *had* to do was to walk up to the little romanesque archway and peer down into the haunting history of those atmospheric grounds. The sunlight danced all the way as far as the eyes could see. I could barely make out the banks of the distant river and the glorious surroundings.

But I just said a quiet "Thank you Owen I know you made this happen for me." And I felt his presence beside me. So too did my friend Pat that morning while we both stood quietly together in the grounds of the old abbey taking in all of its breadth taking and peaceful splendour. Of all the times that I can remember this was the first time I had actually expressed a wish to myself so strongly to visit this place. And whichever way you want to look at it or attach logic to what happened, it does make you think that we are guided every step of the way. And we are also being listened to.

When possible our wishes are sometimes granted in convoluted and interesting ways. There is no rhyme or reason to why they happen but they do. From the simplest to the most complex of events – they happen for us. 'Life happens when we stop making plans...' And I am proof of that. All through that morning I felt his presence and it was wonderful. Some may dismiss what happened as being mere chance but I *know* chance had nothing to do with it. It was orchestrated from a higher power and I had my few moments in one of my very favourite places. Sign posts are all around us. We just have to *see* them and not merely look. It reminds me in early spring when people are so busy with their lives, nature is awakening all around them. The beauty of the cherry blossoms, the daffodils heralding the new season and the flowering bulbs unveiling their first splashes of greenery. Everyone looks at them but not that many take the time to take *time out* and *see* their magnificence. If we all take some time out to listen and look out for signs, they are all around us if we just take a few moments. We owe it to ourselves and to those who we loved when they were alive and with us in this life. The possibilities are endless and we need to learn the art of being patient. For the important things in our life we need to take this valuable 'time out.' I call it 'A time out, to *tune* in.' Even the president of the United States makes time to go for his daily jog. And we would agree that he is at the very least one of the busiest people on the planet. So if he can make this 'time out' then so can you. And if you are busier then he is I take my hat off to you. Life can be very strange. Fascinating too.

If my husband had not died at such a young age, I would not have found myself on this journey of discovery and exploration. The question of "Why are we here?" "What is this place we call life all about?" Age old questions from time immemorial which have been asked and researched and pondered by young and old alike. We may never get the full answers to our questions, but we can at least try. By asking we are expanding our consciousness of the unknown. As I mentioned before my story is my personal one. And my experiences have been both intriguing and enlightening. They are subjective I am conveying them as they happened. Some people prefer not to delve too much into the grey area which comes after we physically die. But for most there is the morbid curiosity at the very least as to what becomes of our consciousness embodiment we know to be you and I. Again matter is never destroyed, it merely changes. There are so many intangible energies around us which we know to be factual but are unable to see with the naked eye. Electricity being one of them. But we also have to be open to the other forces around us which we are not fully able to explain using known scientific methods. In time I do believe we will be further along the path to unlocking the mysteries between this life and the next.

OWEN WALSH
Piano Recital
Painting the Picture with Sound

Venue: Airfield Trust
          Upper Kilmacud
          Dundrum
          Dublin 14

Date: Friday and Saturday
        27th and 28th January 200

Time: 8.00 p.m.

Price: €15.00 & €12.00

*wen Walsh paints a different picture showing us
ow closely our lives are connected to the music
of Debussy Haydn Chopin and many more.*

This was the advertisement cover for Owen's Solo Debut
Concert in Airfield House, in Stillorgan in Dublin. Here
he told the story of the 'Musical Greats' and he performed
their works with emotion and passion to the audience. But
unbeknown to both himself and us all, he was also telling the
story of his own life even up to the very end. This was taken
just two weeks before he died.

Chapter 19

A FATHER'S LOVE

"Hope is hearing the melody of the future;
Faith is dancing to it today."
R.A. Alvez.

We have all heard the stories and investigations of various groups throughout the world undergoing extensive studies on the paranormal and particularly on the Afterlife. Some are better at others in their findings and manner in which they explore this area and the intensity of their endeavours. However, there was one such group of people who over fifteen years in a small town in Britain called Scole. For five years twice a week the group would meet in a small cellar. Robin and Sandra Foy. And Diana and Alan Bennett two of Britain's most accomplished mediums. This was back in 1993. The Bennetts would go into trance and allow the dead to speak through them. As well as their weekly meetings and their own intensive research, they had heard of a gentleman in Italy called Marcello Bacci. Bacci claimed that he could hear the voices of those who had passed on through his old Vacuum Tube Radio. His form of mediumship is called ' Direct Radio Voice (DRV). This is an extremely rare form of mediumship. And is virtually unknown to the public. The Scole Researchers from Britain were wondering if they could communicate themselves through his radio. He conducts regular sessions especially with grieving parents. Parents clearly recognize the voices as belonging to their departed children. Scientists have subjected Bacci's mediumship to a batch of scientific tests. Paolo Pressi was one of the leading Italian investigators. He and his colleagues from El laboratorio an organisation that uses the most stringent methods of science to investigate paranormal claims using software endorsed by the Federal Bureau of Investigation (FBI). El laboratorio have conducted Voice Print Analysis. Like a finger print, a voice print is unique. It can therefore be used to determine someone's identity with near certainty. They compared voice prints from two audio samples. One was the voice print of a young woman called Chiara Lenzi before she died. The other came out of Bacci's radio after her death and was clearly recognised by her father. The comparison produced a ninety seven per cent match. At one stage, Bacci's radio was put inside a special device which shielded it from all radio signals. Yet still the voices continued. At another time the radio was switched off and still the voices were going through it. The third and main point which makes this even more fascinating was the fact that at a later stage the tubes or valves of the radio were totally removed. And still the voices were able to come through .

The Paranormal is that mysterious area behind the seen and the known world. And since most of the world is both unseen and unknown and a good percentage of the world is full of mystery, it is a fascinating area which needs further scrutiny. The only way to have a scientific understanding of more knowledge in this area is to do the research. Professor Archie Roy who is an astronomer and specializes in the movement of celestial bodies, had a discussion with the 'Other Side' about 'Celestial Mechanics. He said that afterwards he thought there were only about half a dozen people in the country who would know exactly what they were talking about. Such evidence is so valuable to research because the mediums would have no academic training in this area. The Scole Group Researchers in Scole in Britain allowed more investigators to scrutinize their sessions. A number of professors from different disciplines were invited. And sometimes they could test their expertise against the expertise on the other side.

Apports also happened regularly in Bacci's center. Apports to refresh your mind is when an object materializes in a room where beforehand was not there. Usually it has some significance to a member present who when their deceased loved one was alive they could identify with this object. It could be a piece of jewellery or a flower or anything which held relevance. It can further substantiate the presence of the person who crossed. Despite the evidence from Scole and Bacci, most scientists still refuse the possibility that consciousness might survive death. Dr. Ruber Sheldrig who is an Internationally renowned biologist and Scole investigator offers an explanation. He says that "There is a dominant materialism in science that grew up in the 19ᵗʰ century. It has become part of the culture of science, but it is really a dogmatic belief system rather then a testable theory. What this means is that scientists have become totally focussed on the things they can both measure and replicate in laboritories. Within science based on the materialist point of view, the mind is the brain. So anything that suggests the mind might be more than the brain goes against the theory and therefore most scientists do not want to know about." - Dr. Rubert Sheldrig.

Another prominent scientist also not convinced that the consciousness is solely the result of brain activity is Dr. Charles Tart. Dr. Tart is a Meritus professor of psychology at the University of California and a leading researcher into the evidence for life after death. He says " The idea that survival of bodily death is impossible and that we are nothing but our brains and bodies is really a function of an out moded view in science. An Utonion World View. This works well for everyday events, but the most interesting thing about modern science, especially when you look at things like Quantum theory is that the world is far more mysterious then we think. He goes on to say: "We now have experimental evidence of what Einstein calls the ("Spooky action at a distance.") i.e. That we can instantaneously effect something in a distant part of the Universe. If Consciousness has any of the qualities of the quantum level of existence, the phenomenon like survival of bodily death are probably not so mysterious after all." Professor Tart has written a book entitled "The End of Materialism." How evidence of the Paranormal is bringing Science and Spirit together. He is internationally known for his psychological work on the nature of consciousness, particularly altered States of Consciousness. He is one of the founders of the field of transpersonal psychology and for his research in scientific parapsychology. He says that genuine science is totally compatible with the Spiritual path. Genuine science arose out of a struggle with repressive religions that told us to believe what they were saying the truth to be. Instead of saying can we not look and go out to see what actually happens in the world. Instead of having to go by authorities. And that is what genuine science is all about. Essential science. The emphasis is on the data. We need an experimental spirituality which can be subject to revision. It should always be open to revision. To being able to allow ourselves to be open to more. He further says that perception is a relatively abitrary construction." And we can apply this to our own everyday interaction with people and situations we find ourselves in. We will always try to use logic and reason to inject into situations which cannot be explained using standard thinking and cognitive reasoning.

And with this in mind it brings me nicely to a time a few years ago concerning my young daughter. At the time she would have been around thirteen or so. And like all children who have lost a parent they can dip into periods of depression and uncertainty. It was on one of these times where she found herself missing her father and feeling a vague sense of hopelessness. This came from the full realisation that she would never again see or hear him in her life in this physical world again. She always wanted him to walk her up the aisle and other precious landmarks which daughters look forward to with their fathers. And she also had the extra burden of being a teen. And like all teenagers they need their fathers every bit as much as they need their mothers. Just in different ways. Combined with this, it is a really tough place to be emotionally despite having any adversity. They are not children nor are they adults. It is the 'transitional stage' which can be extremely confusing to them. Finding their identities and trying to make sense of the world around them. Then throw something like the death of a parent into the mix and the result can be very devastating. During this time she was beginning to question the possibility of an afterlife. Would she ever see him again? When she would speak to him in her quiet moments she said it was just like talking to a wall. She could not *feel* anything. And I could understand that. It is very hard since we are in a physical world and since this is all that we know to grasp anything other then this reality. However, on this particular night before she went asleep she asked her father for a sign. Any sign. To show he was around her. Her desperation trying to cling to whatever she could find. She said what she needed to say then switched off the light to go asleep and hoping that the day ahead would not have as much pain and sorrow. But it arrived with a message and great hope!

The following morning was uneventful. She got herself ready for school as per normal. Got dressed and had her breakfast and prepared for the day ahead in school. As she left and gave me a kiss, I noticed that she was still feeling a little down and despondent. I had no knowledge that the night before she had asked her father for a sign, any sign to let her know that he was around her. It was only when she returned from school and the first thing she did was to question me if I had put anything in her school bag. "Yes, I put your lunch in your bag." "Did you put anything else though?" she enquired further. "No, only your lunch why?" And then she proceeded to tell me that the previous night she was feeling very down about not having her dad and she had asked him to send her some sign to let her know he was still around her. "Do you know what happened when I opened my bag this morning in school for my first lesson?" she said. At this stage I was a little bewildered as I had never seen her excited like this. It was a mixture of amazement and disbelief. "I opened my bag and *this* fell out!" She showed me what was causing her excitement. It was a little leaflet which my husband had inside an old VHS video he had of a classical pianist. He used to watch this hoping to improve his own technique. I remember it but had not seen it for a few years! Again she asked me to swear that I had not placed this in her bag and I reinforced the fact that I had definitely not put this in her school bag. I also told her that I had not seen this leaflet for several years and would not know where to find it even if I wished to get it. Shortly before his death, my husband was preparing to play his own Solo Concert debut in Classical Piano in an evening of "Chopin". It was entitled *"Painting the picture with sound."* He was to play several pieces by Chopin. Both Waltzs and Mazurkas by Chopin. There were many other pieces by different composers he was also to perform like Bach, Haydn, Faure, John Field, Edvard Grieg, Claude Debussy amongst others. So he payed great attention to detail when he practiced these pieces. He was such a perfectionist and this being his first concert ever he really wanted to make a wonderful first impression on everyone who attended. One such classical pianist he observed when he practiced was Kyrstian Zimerman.

Zimerman played Chopin and Schubert in the video. And what fell out of her bag was this very leaflet which used to be inside the jacked cover of the old video which I had not seen for such a long time. The title was 'Krystian Zimerman plays Chopin and Schubert'. It also featured a distinguished photograph of the musician with his artistic hair, and wearing a tuxedo on the cover. Well I certainly was perplexed to say the least. I knew I did not put this into her school bag. And nobody else could have done so either. It was a puzzle and we were both very curious as to how it found its way into the bag. I had packed her lunch the previous night and had closed her bag. I certainly never remember seeing the leaflet in question. The only explanation I can say is that somehow, some *way* which is beyond anything I can explain is that it was put there by her father.... It was her sign and hers alone. Again it is not logical. I am still unable to explain it. But I just accept that these things can and do happen when we least expect them to. Just accepting this brings its own peace. A quiet sense of closure. It again validates that we are not alone. To try and attach logic is futile. Because the more one tries to explain the inexplicable, the further we can push away the answer. By this I mean in human terms and language we as mortals can only understand. But as I mentioned before, these things are beyond human understanding. Acceptance is the only way we can admit that there is something greater than the *known* and tangible substance of this our physical world. And I think if we take this stance it is incredibly consoling and immensely comforting don't you think? To be able to accept that there is more to what we see and what we can explain. That there is a higher power at work. Why do we always have to have the answers? Because some things just go beyond the laws of nature and science. Yes we should accept but not to dismiss what it is we are unable to explain. It certainly fuels our curiosity and I know I want to learn more for whatever time I have left in this dimension.

Both my daughter and I have accepted this and just feel a sense of gratitude that we have both in our own individual ways been touched by this higher force. We have to keep on looking for and asking for signs from those who have crossed over. They can be all around us. If you are only open to accepting that this physical existence which is all we know, to be the only one, then we shut out the many signals around us which are trying to capture our attention no matter how brief that may be. Materialists will argue otherwise but their minds remain closed despite the evidence which the scientific world is revealing. With better technology and advancements in science we are more able then ever to explore and study the uncharted waters of the paranormal and what lies beyond. We will never stop. It was and always will be the age old question as to what happens to us when we die. This physical life is too complex and too precious to be just born, live and end up in total oblivion. It would be so senseless. There has to be a reason for our existence beyond this mere fact of birth, life and death. We are each one of us unique beings. We have our own finger prints completely unique to no other person on the planet. So think about it. You are literally one in seven billion!

Krystian Zimerman
PLAYS CHOPIN & SCHUBERT

This was the leaflet my daughter Sophia found in her school bag. The previous night she had been desperate for her father to give her a sign to show her that he was still with her. The next morning when she arrived in school and opened her school bag she found the leaflet below. I had not seen this in several years and to this day both my daughter and I do not know how it came to be there. I do believe we were witness to an apport. This is the paranormal transference or appearance of an object. There is no other explanation.

Chapter 20
GLIMPSES OF ETERNITY

"We are all here for some special reason. Stop being a prisoner of your past. Become the architect of your future."
- Robin Sharma.

Isn't it interesting how certain experiences which touch our life can have a greater relevance to us at a later stage. At the time we do not pay much heed to. I remember speaking to my friend Pat who is a Chaplain and has tremendous wisdom and faith, telling me some time back about an interesting occurrence which happened to a patient of hers. This incident at the time although fascinating I had put it to the back of my mind. And it is only when I began to write my book that I have heard similar accounts of this incident happening to many others. Briefly she mentioned to me that this elderly married couple were one evening sitting alone together in their living room. The husband was reading across the room from his wife and she was watching the television. Periodically she would look across and speak to him. Nothing strange you might say about that. However, something made her look directly over at her husband at this precise moment and she noticed a grey mist-like cloud leave his head and enter through the ceiling above his body. When she spoke to him again to say what she had seen he did not reply. She repeated her sentence and noticed that he was slightly more slumped in his chair. Upon walking over to him she realised that he was deceased and she was in complete shock. Then she remembered what she had seen only moments before to which she was trying to convey to her husband without knowing he had passed. She said that what she had witnessed must have been his spirit leaving his physical body. And it so happened by chance at just the right moment that she had looked at her husband's body to tell him something. She was able to see the life force leave at the exact moment like a misty grey cloud and go up and out through the top of the room directly above his body.

I was not present with my husband at the point of his death and I honestly believe that if I was meant to be I would have been. Everything happened so quickly and there was so much chaos that it was not possible for me to be present at the *exact* moment. And I know we are all different, but looking back then I think it would have been incredibly difficult to have witnessed his last breadth. Now so many years later and the enlightenment I have encountered along my journey, I think I would be stronger and more able to be present. But each one of us is different and we all have our own strengths and opinions on this question to be present or not with our loved ones at the moment of their death. Nothing is your truth until you experience it for yourself. The skeptics will argue in relation to 'Near Death Experiences' that what the person is going through is the product of a dying brain. The famous 'tunnel of light' reported world wide, and seeing and hearing figures and music from a different realm and so on. But what about the phenomenon of a "*Shared Death Experience*." This is where a bystander will actually witness exactly what the dying person *sees* or *hears*. And there is nothing wrong with *their* brains. They are not experiencing oxygen deprivation or any other kind of physiological changes which may be indicative of a dying body. So this is not so easily explained away as the materialists would like to believe and it is more common then you might think. There can be more then one person present and they can all simultaneously witness the same experience. Just by being in close proximity to a dying loved one. It is better circumstantial evidence.

I believe people who are witness to this are very privileged during this life-death transition. They are usually very emotionally connected to the dying person. But we do not all get to *see* this and it does not mean that our connection was any less then those who do witness this. Some do and some do not and that is just the way it is. I think it would be so reassuring though if we were all to be able to see this, that is those of us who would want to and are open to the afterlife. Such consolation is in itself incredible to be able to see that your relative/friend still lives on just in a different way. This would be a great contribution along the road to recovery in grief management. Again I can think back to the days before my husband passed and I sensed a *stillness* around him and a *feeling* that he was moving on somewhere but at the time I payed very little heed to these feelings. But yes I was picking up something around him. Dr. Raymond Moody's continuing research of NDEs led him to this phenomenon of the 'Shared Near Death Experience'. He had experience with his own mother during her own passing when he was at her bedside. He felt that the actual geometry of the room had changed. Instead of it being a box shape it began to change into something resembling and hour glass shape. This has also been reported by other people. Some have reported seeing a 'portal' open up within the room as if from another dimension and seeing a deceased family member come to meet the person who is passing over. These events cannot be dismissed out of hand. We need to heighten our awareness to what is happening around us in situations like these. The more people who come forward and report their stories the more we need to pay attention and learn acceptance to the wonder and magnificence of this phenomenon.

Dr. Melvin Morse wrote a book entitled "Parting Visions." In the next excerpt he mentions an incident encountered by one of Germany's top poets called Karl Skala. During World War 2, he had a Near Death Experience. "He and his best friend were together in a foxhole during an artillery bombardment. The shells hit closer and closer until one finally hit close to Skala's friend and killed him. Karl felt his friend slump forward into his arms and go limp with death. Then a strange thing happened to Skala. He states that he felt himself being drawn up with his friend, above their bodies and then above the battlefield. Skala could look down and see himself holding his friend. Then he looked up and saw a bright light and felt himself going towards it with his friend. He then stopped and returned to his body. He was uninjured except for a hearing loss that resulted from the artillery blast". (Morse, Parting Visions)

Another type of shared death experience is called the "Shared Deathbed Vision". These are visions that dying people have that are shared with others who are in close proximity to the person about to die. Some see an ethereal body replica of the deceased person lift out of their body. It can sit up or just lift up and out of the room. Because this has been seen by more than one person having observed this, it is classified as a Shared Deathbed Vision. How spectacularly comforting to see such a sight. Imagine the intensity of the observer's emotion just think about it. Unfortunately we are not all privy to this consoling encounter. But we can take comfort by acknowledging those who were honoured to the witnessing departure of their loved ones' spirits. I was twenty two when my paternal grandmother passed on. And I will always remember my mother telling me something unusual as she stood at her bed shortly after she passed.

She had arrived with my father shortly after she died. The hospital had phoned and I had answered. They had informed me that she had just died and my parents at the time were out. So after they arrived home and I had informed them of the call they immediately left the house to go to the hospital. When my mother went into the room and stood at the side of the bed, she told me that she very clearly could see a tiny round bright light like a diamond immediately to the right of my grandmother's head. It stayed there for several moments and then vanished. Perhaps it was her Spirit or someone else's helping her on her way. But it had quite an effect on my mother. She did not find it frightening or disturbing, just extremely interesting. Music has also been heard within rooms not from any physical source and light changes have also been encountered by observers close by. It is all profound and something to think about and not to dismiss. It is also much better the way the medical profession have structured the dynamics of letting family and friends be with the terminally sick especially close to the end. Years ago it was only the doctors or nurses who quietly ushered out family members so they would not be present at the end and witness the final moments of their kin. That has thankfully all changed. And it is primarily because of these changes that people are more able to encounter these special moments of insight and glimpses into the next life. Although nurses especially in hospices will also be able to relate similar experiences as the nature of their work is dealing with the very sick on a regular basis. So the notion that the brain is dying and hallucinations are nothing other than the by-product of a dying anatomy does not hold up. Bystanders who are at the bedside are not dying and they can share similar occurrences so it cannot be explained away as easily as that would you agree?

My own next door neighbour Kay had an interesting and thought provoking experience when her own mother was lying sick in hospital. She began by telling me that on this particular day while she was standing by her kitchen window, the light outside darkened very rapidly and at the same time a flickering shape began to move and float upwards. "As I was looking out of my window and observing this, I immediately thought about my mother and knew at that time she had died." I became very shaken and began to cry. Shortly afterwards a relative called to the house to convey the passing of her mother. When seeing her distressed state thought she had already been informed. Kay said to the person "I know what you have come to tell me, my mother has died hasn't she?" This was then confirmed. Even though she was not in close proximity to her mother when she died what happened to her while she stood by her window had conveyed this to her with a strong *knowing*. She had been home and her mother was in hospital. So they were both physically separated. The person who called did confirm the time her mother had died. It coincided with the same time she had been standing by her kitchen window looking out at the landscape in front of her and seeing it change quite dramatically.   There was a distinctive correlation between what she was observing and the timing of her mother's passing. John Stewart Bell's Theorm – Reality is non- local. There is a hidden world beneath pheomomena. This would explain what was happening to my neighbour in relation to this concept.

Our awareness is able to transcend our ordinary understanding of distance. We all have a second kind of consciousness. Our subliminal self which can respond to any sensory stimuli below our personal levels on consciousness perception. This self is also in touch with the cosmic reality and other realities around us. It can communicate with us on levels we do not undertake or necessarily understand on a conscious level. There are supernormal perception and supernormal means of communication which goes above our physical reality. And this is the hidden world beneath pheomomena. Many of us can relate to this. Time and distance does not in any way stop this kind of connecting with one another. You can be thousands of miles away from a loved one and you *receive* a knowing that all is not well. It can be in a form of a dream or like what occurred with my neighbour Kay and her mother. It is a world we know very little about. Again this could also tie in with intuition. Something in your psyche is 'twigged' or tuned in to that which is outside the five senses we know and understand. You are not your body. We now know that with all the many many hundreds of out of body and near death experiences reported from every corner of the globe. The brain merely facilitates or filters consciousness. It is not its creator. This can be proven when there is no brain function and your heart is stopped. *But*, it is at this time the people who have left their bodies report feeling *more* alive than ever! Your body is in your field of consciousness. Consciousness always proceeds form. And as you learn to activate your Intuition, you bring form and structure out of Consciousness. Our Consciousness connects us to this life at this moment in time.

"My religion consists of a humble admiration of the Illimitable Superior Spirit who reveals himself in the slight details we are able to perceive with our frail and feeble mind." - Albert Einstein.

Illimitable here meaning limitless, boundless, and immeasurable. However, it is in fact the truth. We know very little. But certainly enough to give us the impetus to move forward and search for more. Carl Jung puts it beautifully when he says that "Your vision will become clear only when you look into your heart. "Who looks outside, dreams. Who looks inside, awakens." We must keep looking and never loose sight of our own goals and the main reason why we are all here and what it is Your goal is while you are alive now. If there is something you would truly like to accomplish and which would benefit you and others try to set that particular goal. Remember what you focus on - Expands. The only thing stopping you from your goals is the belief you can or cannot do it. Both are correct! It is your perception to the situation which becomes your own truth. Einstein puts this into effect wonderfully when he says -

Everything is energy and that is all there is to it. Match the frequency of the reality you want and you cannot help but get that reality. It can be no other way. This is not philosophy. This is physics." - Albert Einstein.

I can vouch for this. When I began to have the idea for this book I knew in my heart it was what I had to do. It felt so right. So strong was the compulsion that it manifested for me very easily. For most of us we look outside for answers when really the answers we seek lie within ourselves. When we have an idea about doing something and you get a tremendous excitement alongside this – you just *know* implicitly that it is the right thing for you. And this is what I felt from the very start with my work on my own book. When all the elements come together like timing, opportunity, self-belief, and motivation to name but a few, your goal or goals as the case may be, will become your reality. It will not be anyone else's only yours. But to try is the key. Our reality is not the solid world you believe it to be. As quantum science now proves, it is comprised of wavelengths of energy *that respond directly to your thoughts.* You are the creator of your life's experience whether you are conscious of it or not.

Chapter 21
MOVING ON

"But though our outward man perish,
yet the inward man is renewed day by day."
Cor. 4: 16

A s I conclude my story and my interpretations to what
has happened in my own life. I am dealing now with the
future possibilities to what happens to us next, I try not
to have any particular conclusions. By this I mean to say that if
I was *stuck* on any one outcome or decision by the mere fact of
doing this, I am shutting out any other potential possibilities. And
this does not purely stop as to how we can theorize a situation,
it also applies to social encounters like when we first meet
someone for the first time. First impressions should not close you
down from delving deeper in getting to know someone better,
especially if those first impressions are negative for whatever
reason. Conclusions about anything close you down to what else
is possible. Simply put, we can miss out on finding a new friend,
new possibilities which could enhance your life and lead to a
more fulfilling future. But in regard to what lies beyond this life, a
closed mind can create a barrier to the endless potential that this
universe has to teach and offer each one of us. We all at different
times can become judgemental and closed minded be it through
lack of information, prejudice or just plain disinterest. We are
not able to see the world as it is, but rather we see the world as
we are from our own conclusions about life. This is usually based
on our personal belief systems and subjective experiences from
our birth to the present moment. We need to be more liberal and
objective in our thinking to aid learning and to move forward in
enlightenment. What have I learned? One main lesson and that is
that we are not our bodies. We are so much more than that. It is
something which enables us to move through this life and absorb
what is happening around us. Also the state of consciousness is
not as straight forward as some may believe.

Consciousness lies within each and every one of us and we identify and believe that we are our body. But it is not who you are it is only a part of what you are. Merely the vehicle. And like any vehicle when you die you park it like you would any mode of transport and get out. It is something we all leave behind. It has served its purpose. No matter what religion you have or do not have for that matter there does appear to be a 'higher level of consciousness' behind all creation. Also we are all connected on a very basic level. When we sleep at night during 'Delta sleep' we can all go into this out of the body state. Most of us do not remember it but some do. It is not a dream it is something apart from a dream. Physically it is the recharging process for our bodies which we get during sleep. And it can also be at this stage where we can *meet* loved ones who have gone before us. I will give you another personal example. A few weeks ago I was having a discussion with my sister in the States about moving on and coming to terms with my situation and talking about my husband. I remember saying to her that alot of the time I am alone but luckily for the most part do not feel lonely. I thought no more about our chat but later that night I had a dream. I saw the face of my husband just his face, and he said to me *"Do not be saying that you are alone, I am always with you."* Then the image of his face came right up to me very large whereby I could see the pores in his skin and the colour of his eyes. He then said *"I will love you forever..."* then the image vanished. It was so powerful that it had woken me up. I sat bolt right up in the bed and looked at the time of my alarm clock – it read 5.50am and I started to cry. I felt such strong emotion. It was SO REAL. Another validation for me. Another contact. I have had too many of these 'encounters' just to glibly dismiss them out of hand. This would be foolish and even tragic. But having this subjective experience does not prove it to anyone else but I now know I do not have to prove anything. It is just not possible in human terms. How can any one of us prove the content matter of a dream?

You cannot. You can merely relay the images or feelings relating to your own interpretation or experience of that dream. It can neither be proven or disproven by anyone else other than yourself. It is all relative to each one of us. Some things in life we do not have to explain. Just try to accept and to learn from them. By not being able to prove it happened should not concern us. To accept and not judge opens us up. All I am doing is passing my encounters on and giving food for thought to those who are still questioning if our loved ones leave us. They NEVER do. We are never alone. Believe me I am a testimony to that. I am learning of a greater Spiritual Reality. We can all tap into it. The need to know more beyond our physical existence. It has enriched my life so much.

Science is not able to prove the subjective experience and therefore would usually exclude it. I have experienced this expanded reality and so too have many other people. Science in the past would usually accept the objective criteria and content. And this being that what you can measure is real and what you can not measure is not there. There may come a point in science where the content of consciousness can be proven or measured. But for the time being all we have now are verbal accounts by people relating their subjective experiences. Most if not all of these seem to have a common thread running through them. For example to name but one out of many. Take the Out of Body or Near Death experiences reported globally by thousands of people. Here we can say that science can take an *objective aspect from a subjective experience* to prove a particular point or reality if you will. A reality which as yet cannot be proven tangibly or in a more structured format. The basis of mind and matter is consciousness. We individualize our consciousness through the filter of our nervous system and our subjective experiences. If you think of a thought universe it is akin to a virtual universe. A conceptual universe. We are all connected. Empathy is one good sign of this.

When dealing in any area where one does not have hard evidence in the tangible sense, it is more difficult to convey and impress with conviction definitive proof to the sceptics and materialists out there who will refute any evidence in the area of the paranormal. But in trying to prove any point we have to become like the positive thinkers out there who *see the invisible, feel the intangible, and achieve the impossible.* With our human nature sometimes the eyes see only what the mind is ready to understand. I do believe and this is just my feeling about the Afterlife, that we have been given little *'tasters'* from beyond. By that I mean that there is *some* evidence but not *sufficient* evidence to show us that yes there is another realm beyond this life we know here as mortals on earth. But here is the thing, perhaps if we were given the sufficient and definitive evidence which we require without a shadow of a doubt, our own individual purpose here would not perhaps progress as it was ordained to be. Our own unique presence here at this moment in time would not probably reach its full conclusion and destiny. We would all want to go to this wonderful place beyond any earthly beauty we could possibly imagine. And our focus would be dulled and distracted. My experiences before and since loosing my husband are subjective. They are my own. But I know they were real. I was not influenced by other people's dogma because like most people I had never experienced what other's had in relation to the Afterlife. I had a certain attitude like us all but it was not until I had experience of my own that I was able to make my own conclusions.

Yes I have been touched by the Otherside and very blessed and privileged that I have been so. I have become deeply Spiritual as a result. And although I can still have moments of loneliness and dispondency, I also have a strong foundation of consoling reassurance. Consolation and comfort to know that this life is not the only one. We do go on. I do believe now that 'death in the physical' is 'birth in the Spiritual'. When we change our attitude - we change our life. This applies to all areas of our lives. Because we owe our comfortable survival here to the five senses which we have. We have the need to *see, to look for,* and *to behold.* Our sense of sight is what most of us depend on for proof. But we should have more *Insight* than *Eyesight*. The intangible cannot be explained tangibly. Not always. Our eyes behold the wonderous complexities of this world. But what our eyes are able to see is but a tiny fraction of all the many frequencies which are present around us in this Universe. Most of it is invisible energy but none the less it is still present. And also not all light frequencies are seen by the naked eye. We are only able to see a small spectrum for example, our eyes neither see Infra-red or Ultra Violet Light. What we call matter is really organised and stable energy. But most of matter is emply space. It is a general term for the substance of which all physical objects exist. It makes our physical world. Then we have energy, information and then mind comes later. This is the Material perspective. Spirit is another type of Energy. We as a species do not like information which we are unable to fully comprehend. Also which may be inconsistent with our own belief systems which may stem from either religious or environmental conditioning handed down from our ancestors. We need to rise above environmental conditioning and programming. Ignore paradigms and look for new ones relative to each one of us. If we fall into the trap of rigid belief systems we become stuck. Having an open mind will expand you to new possibilities and opportunities. And belief systems are crucial to filtering reality. Again we now know that the mind and brain are separate. They are not the same. Brain function is separate from mind and consciousness. Near Death and Out of Body experiences have gone into great detail with case studies to demonstrate this. And the scientists are now acknowledging this. Dr. Peter Fenwick goes into great detail about the mind being separate from the brain and consciousness in his book "The Art of Dying."

There is also a study for those who would like more evidence in this area called "The Aware Study." And of course I have found once you begin to talk about this subject to others, you will immediately get people opening up and sharing their own personal paranormal experiences. Or telling of someone close to them who has gone through a similar event. I have found this to be the case in many social encounters. It is a lot more common than one would think. The days are thankfully long gone when people whispered quietly to one another if they had something *unusual* they were unable to explain. The 'giggle factor' among professionals is also diminishing. Because too many people have and are still coming forward to tell their own stories across the globe. And who are we to dismiss them all out of hand as delusional or 'out of their mind'. And that expression 'out of the mind' does indeed have strong significance and relevance to NDEs or OBEs if taken literally. They are literally more out of their bodies than out of their minds. Their minds have indeed gone elsewhere to some other realm or dimension. But they are very grounded people who have experienced a new sense of reality. Those with a 'closed mind' are therefore incapable of having 'an open mind'. And consequently dismiss the rest of us as being 'out of our minds '! An outdated and outmoded reaction thankfully becoming less frequent. But I truly hope that what I have been talking about in this book will open more minds - just a little. Dr. Mario Beauregard – neuroscientist and author of 'The Spiritual Brain' has penned his new book entitled 'Brain Wars.' In this book he also goes into great detail demonstrating that scientific materialism is false and that the mind and consciousness are not simply electrochemical processes taking place in the brain. Logically we know that there has to be an intact neural network required for our consciousness to function and to be. But how is it then that people who have clinically *died* and have come back to life with memories and are able to relate incidents within the operating room be explained? Their brain function had stopped but their thinking continued. The answer is we simply do not know. We have the data but not the explanation. There are speculations but no comprehensive definitive theory.

We in the western world derive our logic from Aristotle's two fold system of logic which is – something is either true or false. And using this model of logic leads us to mysteries which we neither can prove or disprove. This is the grey area between the two. So for the moment we as people need to have a new way of thinking. There is so much room for expansion. Expansion of ideas, theories and a more condensed focus into the study of the unknown without prejudice and that is very important. Again the open mind is crucial.

Montague 'Monty' Keen was a member of 'The Society for Psychical Research' for over fifty years. He was the leading investigator in the 'Scole Experiments' from 1993 – 1998. And also a leading investigator into the area of life after death. He saw the quality of the available evidence out there improving and expanding. He agreed that materialism was becoming outdated because of strong evidential information being given by people who had been contacted by loved ones and had witness to inexplicable phenomena. The sceptics and the believers will forever bicker and disagree with one another in this field. For the sceptics the *grey* area does not exist. It is either black or white. They are steadfast in their own convictions and belief systems. But as Montague Keen said and I quote:

"The sceptics regard the possibility of the survival of the

human consciousness as inherently so impossible

that anyone must be rather crazy to believe it. But

when you look at the evidence you have to ask

yourself whether you would be even more crazy not

to believe it or to find some alternative explanation

which makes any sort of sense and I haven't found one."

I will continue to embrace what I have learned and will hopefully experience more wonderous and momentous signs and connections which will further validate my own conviction that this journey here called life is just the beginning. And I would like to give the final word to my husband Owen who used to say so many many times while he was alive the following quote that:

"We are only passing through here,
The BEST is yet to come ...."

And finally I would like to include here the poem which I had started at the beginning of my book. I am very sure that if our loved ones could verbally communicate with us all it is the following words they would quickly convey with conviction, joy and love.

To My Dearest Family.

*Some things I'd like to say but first of all to let you know that
I arrived okay
I'm writing this from Heaven where I dwell with God above
Where there are no more tears or sadness, its just eternal love
Please do not be unhappy just because I'm out of sight
Remember that I'm with you every morning, noon and night.*

*That day I had to leave you when my life on earth was
through
God picked me up and hugged me and He said I welcome
you
It's good to have you back again you were missed while you
were gone
As for your dearest family they'll be here later on
I need you here so badly as part of My big plan
There's so much that we have to do to help our mortal man*

*Then God gave me a list of things He wished for me to do
And foremost on that list of mine is to watch and care for
you
And I will be beside you every day and week and year
And when you're sad I'm standing there to wipe away the
tear
And when you lie in bed at night the day's chores put to flight
God and I are closest to you in the middle of the night*

*When you think of my life on Earth and all those loving
years
Because you 're only human they are bound to bring you
tears
But do not be afraid to cry it does relieve the pain
Remember there would be no flowers unless there was some
rain
I wish that I could tell you of all that God has planned
But if I were to tell you wouldn't understand*

But one thing is for certain though my life on Earth is o're
I am closer to you now than I ever was before

And to my very many friends trust God knows what is best
I'm still not far away from you I'm just beyond the crest
There are rocky roads ahead of you and many hills to climb
But together we can do it taking one day at a time

It was always my philosophy and I'd like it for you too
That as you give unto the World so the World will give to you
If you can help somebody who is in sorrow or in pain
Then you can say to God at night my day was not in vain

And now I am content that my life it was worth while
Knowing as I passed along the way I made somebody smile
So if you meet somebody who is down and feeding low
Just lend a hand to pick them up as on your way you go

When you are walking down the street and you've got me on
your mind
I'm walking in your footsteps only half a step behind
And when you feel the gentle breeze or the wind upon your
face
That's me giving you a great big hug or just a soft embrace

And when it's time for you to go from that body to be free
Remember you're not going you are coming here to me
And I will always love you from that land way up above
Will be in touch again soon.

P.S. God sends His Love.

THE END

Bibliography

Dr. Thomas Campbell – My Big T.O.E.   Chapter 8.

Rickard and Kelly – Photographs of the Unknown.

Virginia Hummel - Miracle Messenger Signs from Above
Love from Beyond. Chapter 9.

Kilner, Walter John (1965) 'The Human Aura.' Chapter 15.

Aine Belton – Matrix Shift – Change your Energy
Change your World. Chapter 17.
.
Max Planck - Quantum Theory. Chapter 17.

Professor Tart - The End of Materialism. Chapter 19.

Dr. Raymond Moody – Life after Life. Chapter 20.

Dr. Melvin Morse – Parting Visions. Chapter 20.

Dr. Peter Fenwick. - The Art of Dying. Chapter 21.

Dr. Mario Beauregard – The Spiritual Brain and Brain Wars.
Chapter 21.